D1266561

Sutherland

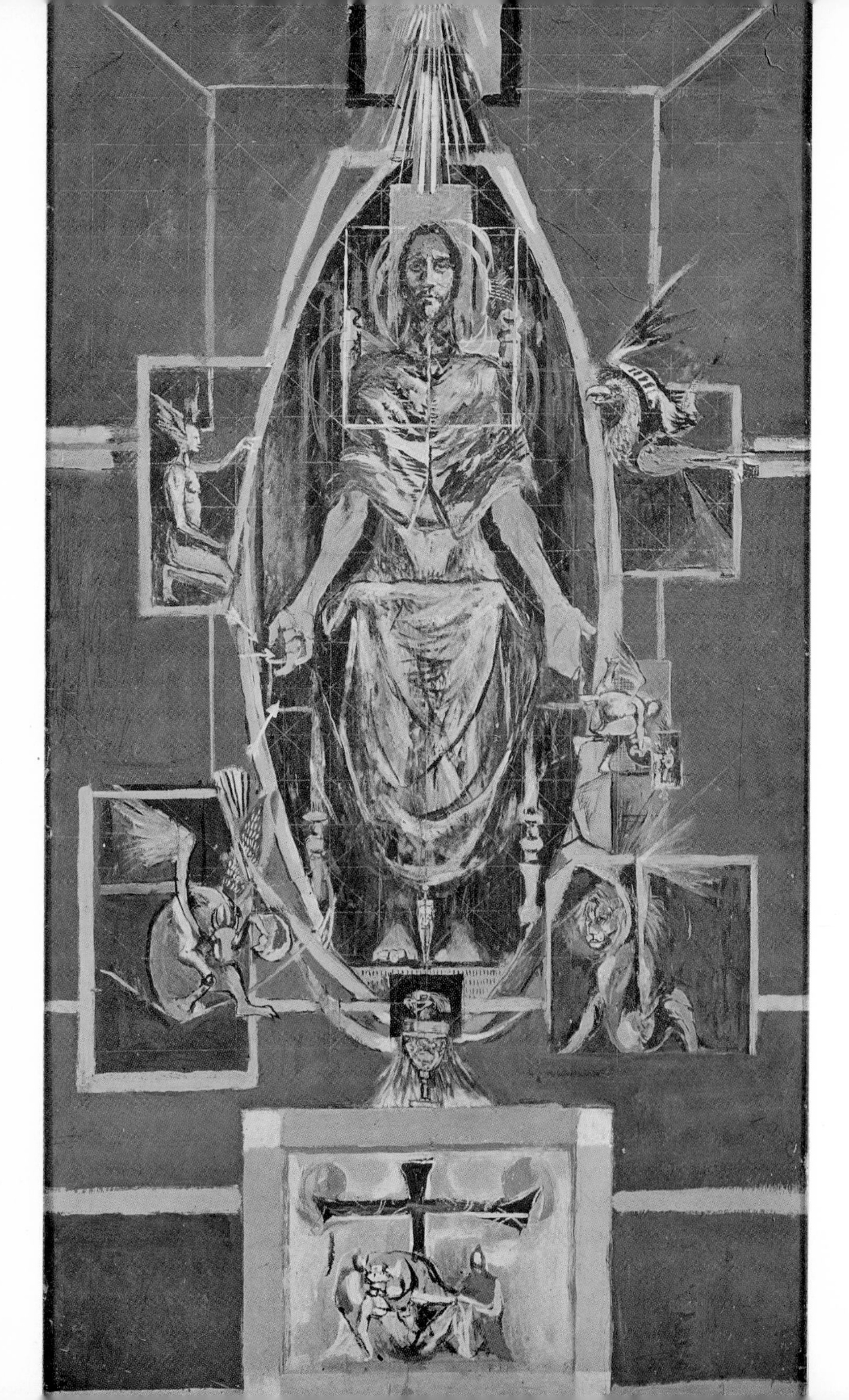

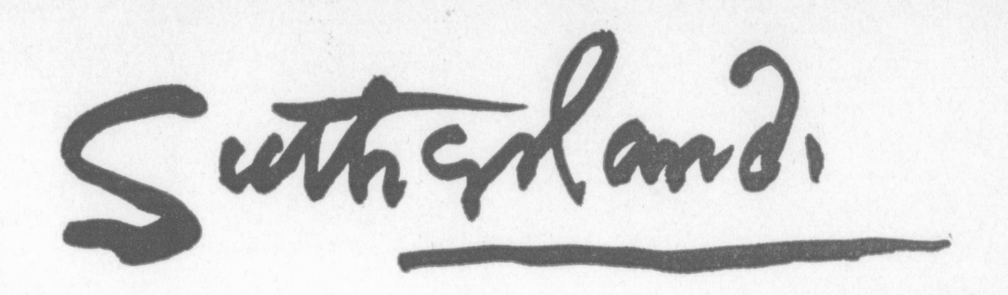

THE COVENTRY TAPESTRY

The Genesis of the Great Tapestry in Coventry Cathedral

"Christ in Glory in the Tetramorph"

TEXT EDITED BY ANDREW RÉVAI

Based on Conversations with the artist

INTRODUCTION BY ERIC NEWTON

NEW YORK GRAPHIC SOCIETY

Greenwich, Connecticut

First published May 1964

Made in Great Britain

Text printed
by William Clowes and Sons, Ltd., London and Beccles
Colour plates printed
by John Swain & Sons, Ltd., Barnet
Photogravure plates printed
by Ets. Braun & Cie., Mulhouse, France
Cover printed in offset lithography
by Curwen Press, Ltd., London,
from an original design by Graham Sutherland

For K.S., Marie Cuttoli and the weavers of Felletin

ACKNOWLEDGMENTS

The Publishers are greatly indebted to Her Majesty The Queen for her gracious permission to reproduce on Plate 5 the preliminary study for the Tapestry from Her Majesty's private collection. Grateful acknowledgments are also due to the Coventry Cathedral Council for their permission to reproduce the final cartoon, the Tapestry and details thereof. Also to the following owners of works illustrated: the Directors of the Redfern Gallery, London, Mr. Rex. de C. Nan Kivell, Mrs. Dorothy Searle and Mr. H. Tatlock Miller; Lady Honor Svejdar, Co. Dublin; Mrs. Alice Hunt, New York; and Mr. and Mrs. John Hunt, Co. Dublin.

The Publishers also wish to thank Sir Basil Spence and Professor Sir Anthony Blunt for having kindly read the manuscript; M. Olivier Pinton of Felletin and Mr. Donald King of the Victoria & Albert Museum for supplying the notes on the weaving; the Photographic Department of the Courtauld Institute of Art at London University for their assistance in undertaking the major part of the black-and-white photography; and P. W. & L. Thompson of Coventry for supplying the colour photographs of the Tapestry.

The drawings embellishing the text have been specially designed for this book by Graham Sutherland.

CONTENTS

INTRODUCTION

Sir Basil Spence's new Cathedral at Coventry, built side by side with the bombed ruins of the old Gothic cathedral and architecturally integrated with them, has not unnaturally attracted the attention of everyone who is interested either in the possibilities of modern architecture or the revival of the religious spirit in twentieth century England. What was unexpected was the startling extent to which the new building—a contemporary phoenix rising out of the ashes of the past—has caught the imagination of the whole country. Ever since the opening ceremony in May, 1962, an endless procession of visitors has passed through the building—statistics estimate the number during the past year at over two million—drawn to Coventry by something more serious than mere curiosity. The Cathedral has, in fact, become a symbol. It is a test of how the vision of a single directing mind, working in close collaboration with a carefully chosen team of artists and craftsmen, could translate the essence of the Christian spirit and Christian ritual, as conceived by the mid-twentieth century, into purely visual terms.

So complex a problem could not be solved easily. Only after frequent discussions and consultations between the architect, the ecclesiastical authorities and the contributing artists over a period of ten years did the building receive its final form: but one decision has remained constant throughout—that on the great wall at the "east" end there should be a dominant and arresting image that would set the mood for the whole interior and would be visible at every point in one's progress from the main entrance at the "west" end to the high altar.* That image, it was ultimately decided, was to be a tapestry covering the whole of the wall—the largest tapestry in existence—and that the commission for the work should be given to Graham Sutherland

That decision was made in 1952 and one purpose of this book is to explain to the reader, by way of a question and answer discussion with the artist, the slow genesis of the work from start to finish, the gradual evolution of the design, the various stages of trial and error in the mind of the artist himself, his attempts to adapt himself to suggestions made, or, at times, his reasoned rejection of such suggestions.

The other purpose is to illustrate, by the long sequence of plates, that same evolution. For who can say, when an artist broods, with his pencil or brush in hand, on the next step in the slow progress of such a work, whether each decision has been taken by the mind or by the eye? The difference between a curve and an angle, between a smooth and a violent transition, can be of the utmost importance in arriving at the final destination. Yet I doubt whether Sutherland's verbal explanations as to how those decisions were arrived at are as charged with meaning as the drawings themselves. In fact I feel certain that the verbal and the visual story

* Spence built the new cathedral on a north-south axis, so that it should connect with the north wall of the ruined old cathedral. Thus what is for liturgical purposes the "east" end of the new cathedral, with the high altar, is in fact geographically the north end.

told in this book reinforce each other so completely that neither would make sense without the other, and that the arrangement of the plates in chronological sequence is as necessary for clarity as the logical sequence of question and answer in the text.

A work so ambitious and so difficult could not be envisaged in a single courageous act of the creative imagination. Only after long and often agonising deliberation could the final result be arrived at. Ideas which seemed at first appropriate and promising were rejected: others took their place and were again either rejected or modified: the modifications were elaborated: colour schemes were chosen and abandoned. But never, in the slow creative process, did the architect, the church authorities or the artist himself lose sight of the central problem. This huge tapestry of an enthroned Christ in Glory surrounded by symbols of the four Evangelists was to carry the main burden of an emotional impact that was to dominate the building and establish a mood to which the whole of the interior was to be subordinated.

Sutherland's statements reveal in considerable detail and, as far as possible, in the artist's own words, the growth and development of this image, not omitting its technical aspects and the part played in it by the weavers at Aubusson who worked so closely with the artist, sometimes influencing him by their expert knowledge of the nature of the medium, sometimes influenced by him when the medium itself seemed to present difficulties that threatened to defeat his intentions.

Such a story cannot fail to shed a light on the creative process that is not often successfully put into words. For Sutherland is a remarkably articulate and self-analytical artist and his interviewer was unusually aware of the kind of question that would provoke the informative answer.

My own purpose in this brief introduction is not so much to intervene between artist and questioner or to comment on their success in making clear the intricate process of gestation, as to see the finished tapestry in relation to previous images that, in the long history of Christian art, have attempted to solve the same problem of translating a deeply felt religious emotion into an effective visual symbol on a scale large enough to be easily read from a distance and yet with sufficient detail and complexity to preserve its meaning, and even to add to it, when seen at close quarters.

Sutherland was from the first, as one can gather from his statements, well aware that such images existed, and that Romanesque artists and architects, especially of the twelfth century, had produced them in plenty. They could be, as he well knew, both an inspiration and a hindrance. Anything as powerful as the great tympanum of the Basilica of Vézelay or as packed with symbols as the scuplture of the Last Judgment at Autun could hardly fail to appeal to a twentieth century artist as tempting prototypes or, at least, as useful foundations on which to build. Yet to pay even mild homage to the twelfth century in a building that so frankly belongs to the twentieth would have been stylistically fatal and artistically insincere, especially when one remembers that in Coventry from the "west" entrance up to the Baptistery, one third of the way to the altar, nothing in the way of decoration or imagery is visible but the tapestry itself. The Cathedral is so designed that nothing is allowed to compete with the tapestry until one is a few yards from the high altar, and even then one has to turn one's back on it in order to examine the ten stained glass windows which are not visible from the "west" door. If it does not make its meaning clear at the first moment, both stylistically and in its religious content (if, indeed, the two can be separated), it has failed in its central purpose. Perhaps the only other equally impressive images to which a modern artist could usefully cast his mind back are the great Pantocrator busts in mosaic (also of the twelfth century) in the semi-domes of the Sicilian churches of Cefalù, Monreale and the Cappella Palatina in Palermo. They are more awe-inspiring, less welcoming than the enthroned Christs of Northern Europe, but they too, are hindrances to an artist of our own day in his attempt to evolve an iconography that will be both meaningful and acceptable to the century we live in.

These are massive difficulties. They are fully explained by Sutherland himself, and his interviewer suggests that perhaps the only other twentieth century artist who could have tackled them would be Rouault. Yet I suggest that Rouault, with his more forceful and direct way of working, might have been baffled by the sheer size of what was required. The immense emotional pressure of his *Miserere* lithographs, enlarged to cover an area 80 feet high and 40 feet wide, would surely have destroyed the sense of scale with which both Spence and Sutherland have been so concerned. Rouault would, I think, have destroyed the relationship between the tapestry and its architectural context and in so doing would have turned the "east" wall at Coventry into a huge illustration to a gargantuan book. Also one wonders whether the tenderness which *must* be fused with the ideas of nobility and omnipotence in such an image would have been within Rouault's range. For Rouault is, to my mind, the kind of artist who depends on the simple, decisive single blow of the hammer that drives the nail straight home without preliminary experimentation. His is the art that refuses to reinforce or dilute a central idea by building subsidiary ideas, however relevant, round it. He is the artist of the bold single statement, not of the huge expanse that is part of a larger concept.

Sutherland's problem throughout has been to add, little by little, to the central idea without diminishing its importance, and this, it seems to me, he has done with great singlemindedness. Remove the "boxes" that contain the emblems of the four Evangelists and the gigantic central figure of Christ would have lost not only its strength but much of its meaning, and not only its meaning but its relationship with the whole interior. One of the factors in the design that makes it "belong" so intimately to its context is the deliberate series of gradations in scale between the relatively small human figure between the feet of the seated Christ, through the Crucifixion at the base of the tapestry, the isolated St. Michael and the four symbols of the Evangelists that build up in a crescendo to the central seated figure of Christ in Glory.

The effect is not merely that of a steady, calculated crescendo in music but also a broadening out of the rhythm, a leading up, without awkward jerks, to the predestined climax—what a composer would describe with the word *allargando*—the whole sequence being firmly tied together by the steady framework of the bands that act as a "mandorla" to the central throne, the "boxes" that hold the four symbols in place and the strong verticals and horizontals that relate the tapestry to the whole of the "East Wall". This—to carry the musical analogy a little further—makes the tapestry symphonic in conception. Rouault's version would have been rhapsodic.

The reader will certainly find the detailed description of how the tapestry gradually assumed its final shape, quite apart from the relationship (largely governed by the sheer *timing* of it) between the artist and the weavers, quite absorbing. Here we are in the realm of fact, and even when the facts may seem odd and surprising in their chronological sequence, this part of the book—the whole of it with the exception of the final chapter—is a straightforward statement of what happened, and as far as I can remember no carefully compiled description of the progress of a long-drawn-out event has attempted such accurate detail. The interval between conception and birth, examined so closely, cannot fail to be both complex and astonishing, and the whole amounts to a struggle between the inevitable pressure of tradition and the determination to evolve a personal image that would not only harmonise with the contemporary spirit of the Cathedral itself but—more important—would be the visual equivalent of his own personal solution of the problem involved. It becomes more and more evident as one reads his account of endless experiments made and abandoned that the struggle was a real and an exhausting one. It reads almost like a round-by-round commentary on a battle of wills. It was not merely a question of balancing aesthetics against a will to communicate a personal message. Phrases like "this interfered, as it turned out, with the essential symmetry of the design" show the temporary victory of tradition: other phrases like "this, in the end, seemed to me hackneyed and sentimental" are evidence of the creative imagination protesting against the seductive influence of prototypes. I can remember no other account of a struggle of this kind in which an artist has deliberately flirted with his own temptations, actually making endless diagrams, quotations as it were, from the past only in order to reject them, as a boxer might study his opponent's technique of attack in order to develop his own line of defence. What other artist would have deliberately drawn up a list of "quotations" which he was determined *not* to use, however effective they might be? Even so would one compile a kind of *index expurgatorius*, a forbidden vocabulary, lest the temptation to use it should prove a hindrance to sincerity. One is reminded of St Thomas's fear, in T. S. Eliot's *Murder in the Cathedral* lest he should "do the right thing for the wrong reason".

I suspect that this fear is the cause of Sutherland's reiterated insistence that he must introduce elements of "the real" into the symbolism in which he was necessarily involved in designing the tapestry. For what was a live symbol in the twelfth century could not fail to become a dead one in the twentieth. The hands and feet of the central figure, the character of the four creatures who, by tradition, symbolise the four Evangelists, must be *seen* as well as understood—"copies", perhaps, from what appeared in the mirror or was observed in the Maidstone Zoo.

This brings me to my own comment on what is, after all, the core of the book and the essence of Sutherland's problem, namely the nature of religious art as such. Both Graham Sutherland and Andrew Révai have approached the problem, as it affects the artist, with immense seriousness. In fact the last chapter of this book could be isolated and regarded as an essay on the theme of the artist in service to his religious creed.

It is certainly not my purpose to intervene between the two authors of this essay, yet I would be evading my own responsibilities in writing this short introduction if I did not state, as briefly and as precisely as possible, my own point of view.

Quite simply, I regard religious art as one that has to pass a fundamental test. It is concerned (and I do not confine this statement to Christian art alone) with the relationship between mankind and his god or gods. And since man is visible, material and tangible and God is invisible—a concept experienced rather than a presence seen—the essence of religious art must lie in its power to distinguish between the seen and the unseeable, between the material and the spiritual, between the natural and the supernatural.

This, the Greeks could not do. We cannot guess whether the archaic statue is an Apollo or a young athlete. Yet even so convinced a materialist as Rembrandt could do it with ease. In his "Adoration of the Shepherds" in the National Gallery, in a barn near Amsterdam, Dutch peasants gather round a newly born babe and we know by some mysterious instinct that the Child is a divine Child who will change the destiny of the world. Matisse cannot make the distinction, nor can Velazquez, nor Caravaggio. Picasso, even though he so rarely makes the specific attempt, can achieve it and in doing so proves himself a religious artist.

In Sutherland's case there can be no doubt. The Northampton "Crucifixion" and the Chichester "Noli Me Tangere" are both, by my test, deeply felt religious works on specifically Christian themes. Yet, because they are personal in conception, traditional forms have played hardly any part in their making.

The Coventry tapestry passes the same test. It too is a truly religious work, though in the case of a work of art so vast and so intimately integrated with its architectural context, echoes of traditional iconography could not be so easily dispensed with. Yet even here the artist has seen to it that tradition exercises no restraint over his creative imagination. He has dispensed with Romanesque devices yet his concern is with the supernatural and his theme is Divinity.

Christianity itself imposes its own limitations which the

Christian artist must obey without losing his freedom as an artist. Even so, a footballer must obey the rules of the game he plays, and in doing so he increases rather than diminishes his own potency as a player. It is the pattern imposed on him by a creed to which he himself subscribes that gives him power. That pattern, for the Christian artist, has been developing ever since the mosaic artists of the mausoleum of Galla Placidia in Ravenna broke away from Hellenistic formulae in the fifth century. It is a pattern onto which every truly religious artist has built his own stylistic additions, and in doing so has enriched it.

If the artist does not realise that styles and traditions change with the centuries, as the relationship between man and God inevitably changes, then the language of religious art will become atrophied and sterile. The purpose of this book, as I see it, is to trace, in considerable detail and with reference to one specific work of art and one specific artist, the change that has taken place during the past decade.

Eric Newton

THE CHALLENGE

TOWARDS THE END OF THE LAST WAR, Canon Walter Hussey, now Dean of Chichester, took the momentous decision of commissioning first Henry Moore and subsequently Graham Sutherland to create two works of art on religious themes to decorate the north and south transepts of the parish church of St. Matthew at Northampton, a late Victorian building erected shortly before the turn of the century in a style described by Nikolaus Pevsner as "big and prosperous". It was thus the vision of the patron rather than this unsympathetic setting which became the point of departure for contemporary religious art in England.

The first major opportunity in England to combine contemporary religious art *and* architecture arose with the rebuilding of Coventry Cathedral, which was destroyed by German bombs in November, 1940. This achievement runs parallel with the first endeavours within the Catholic Church to promote modern sacred art in France as exemplified above all by the church of Assy. These were inspired by the Dominican order, which also embarked on the worker-priest movement aimed at freeing the Church from its self-imposed isolation. Both these initiatives of the Dominicans met with the strongest disapproval on the part of the official Church.

In 1947 the Commission set up to consider the reconstruction of Coventry Cathedral produced a report recommending an architectural competition with the proviso that the design should be in the Gothic style. In 1950, however, when the conditions for the competition were announced, this stylistic proviso was abandoned. In fact, no stipulations were laid down, thus making it possible for the new cathedral to be conceived entirely in contemporary terms. The results of the competition, in which 219 architects participated, were announced in August, 1951. The Reconstruction Committee accepted the project put forward by Spence (now Sir Basil Spence) of preserving the ruins of the old Gothic cathedral and erecting adjacent to these a new building in simple contemporary style. The concept of the Great Tapestry already figures in Spence's report attached to his design, worded as follows:

> "*The Tapestry*. The tapestry is backed by a stone wall, and is hanging from great bronze pins built into the wall. This tapestry, for which £30,000 has been allowed in the estimate, could be designed by a great contemporary artist, or a competition might be organised and the firm who exhibited modern tapestries in the recent Arts Council Exhibition in London has been approached, and has the necessary scope to undertake the commission. This would be the largest tapestry in the world, and would be the most beautiful background for the altar and the charred cross. The subject of the tapestry is the Crucifixion."

Sir Basil, in his book on the building of the cathedral,* recalls that at the time of the announcement of the competition he had

* Basil Spence, *Phoenix at Coventry*, London, 1962.

already decided that, if his plan were accepted, he would invite Graham Sutherland to design the Great Tapestry. Accordingly, at one of the early meetings of the Reconstruction Committee towards the end of 1951, he asked for permission to approach Sutherland. In the meantime, however, the proposed subject-matter had changed, and the suggestion finally put forward to Sutherland was not for a Crucifixion but for a Christ in Glory, illustrating Chapter IV, verses 2, 3, 6 and 7 of the Book of Revelation.

Spence's conception of the tapestry as the dominant feature of the cathedral's interior again forms an interesting parallel with Assy, the apse of which is filled with Lurçat's tapestry of the apocalyptic vision. The conception of translating the creative artist's cartoon into its final state by the craftsman also ran parallel with the example of Assy, where the principal pictorial decoration consists of the mosaic designed by Léger for the building's façade, Lurçat's tapestry for the apse, the ceramic murals and tiles designed by Chagall and Matisse, and the stained glass designed by a number of artists including Rouault. Thus both Assy and Coventry provide examples of reviving the *artisanat* for modern church art.

In medieval times, tapestries were manufactured as mobile decorations which were transportable from one castle to another, and which were easily hung up and taken down as church adornments on feast days. Spence, however, conceived the Great Tapestry for the new Coventry Cathedral as a permanent feature, not only for aesthetic but also for practical reasons, since a large expanse of woven material would play an important part in the improvement of the acoustics. He accordingly wrote to Sutherland on November 22nd, 1951, inviting him to design the tapestry (see

Appendix I). Sutherland replied guardedly and suggested a meeting, which took place on January 5th, 1952, at Villefranche. After discussions lasting a week, he accepted the invitation in principle and the official commission was embodied in a letter from the Reconstruction Committee dated January 16, 1952.

Sutherland was fully aware of the challenge which this commission set him and in fact the problems of the tapestry's design and execution were to preoccupy him for the next ten years. One of the main difficulties for contemporary artists who approach religious subject-matter is, as Douglas Cooper put it in his perceptive analysis of Sutherland's religious painting, that "they must first decide whether they will dare to leap the barriers and invent a contemporary stylistic formula for traditional Christian subjects, thereby perhaps giving them renewed life and actuality, or whether they feel obliged to try to reconcile their own vision with an accepted formula in the hope of being able to achieve an up-to-date compromise".*

In his other works, as a landscape painter, war artist, portraitist and painter of commissioned and non-commissioned religious subjects, Sutherland never had to face the same difficulties as with this tapestry. First, there were the limitations as to subject-matter, laid down by the patrons and drawn up in a statement by Provost Howard on December 22nd, 1951 (see Appendix II). Although the patrons, the Bishop and Provost of Coventry, as well as the Reconstruction Committee, showed great sympathy with Sutherland's concept, they tried, even as late as 1957, to induce him to accept subjects for the lower panel which were unsympathetic to him (see Appendix III, letter from the Provost dated April 17th, 1957).

* Douglas Cooper, *The work of Graham Sutherland*, London, 1961.

Unlike the Northampton Crucifixion, the subject of Christ in Glory was not of Sutherland's own choosing, yet he took up the challenge of depicting anew a subject which had formed the principal theme of Christian art for many centuries, from Byzantine times, throughout the 9th-century Carolingian renaissance, down to the pictorial and sculptural decorations of Romanesque churches. This was based on Chapter IV of the Book of Revelation in which St. John sees Christ in Glory seated on a throne, encompassed by a rainbow and surrounded by the four beasts. St. John goes on to describe in Chapter V how Christ holds in His right hand the book with seven seals. This Christ in Majesty surrounded by a mandorla became the prototype of representations of Christ in Glory in the Tetramorph right down to the Middle Ages.

But which representation should Sutherland look to for inspiration? Each epoch in both East and West developed its own way of interpreting this theme. The Pantocrator of Byzantine art, Christ the All-Ruler, was a specifically eastern conception of Christ uniting in Himself the first and second persons of the Trinity, depicted in the bust-length medallions in Byzantine churches as the apocalyptic judge who, on the last day, opens the book in His right hand. Alternatively, the traditional representation in western art of

Christ in Majesty shows Him as a full-length figure, now God, now King, seated on the throne, holding the book in His right hand and raising His left hand in blessing. Then again, with the approach of the expected Millennium, representations of Christ at the Day of Judgment became one of the most popular themes of church art; in this interpretation, based on Revelation, Chapter XX, and St. Matthew, Chapter XXV, Christ the Judge does not hold the book, nor is He always seated, but either spreads out His hands or holds them upraised, mostly spreading them out in a gesture of receiving the blessed whilst the guilty perish in hell-fire.

The large number of historical antecedents, both in East and West, were bound to complicate Sutherland's attempts to achieve a concept of his own expressed in contemporary terms. Moreover his patrons, however understanding they were, could not help seeking to impose their views even as to style: thus Provost Howard, after seeing the first cartoon, wrote to Sutherland on September 1st, 1953: "The face of Christ is going to be your greatest work and I am sure you will succeed. Victory, serenity, and compassion will be a great challenge to combine. Just as the Italians boldly conceived an Italian face for Christ and the Spanish a Spanish face, it may come to you to conceive of an English face, universal at the same time."

Apart from the problems posed by subject and style, there was also the task of harmonising the tapestry with its architectural surroundings. Sutherland and Spence worked in the closest consultation, yet changes in the shape and scale of the building, in the material and colouring of the setting, made it necessary for Sutherland to search for new formulas and solutions. Finally, there were the difficulties of the scale and medium.

It is therefore not surprising that Sutherland had to do far more preliminary studies for the Great Tapestry than for any other of his works. He made hundreds of sketches, both for the whole composition and for individual motifs. Many of these he destroyed, but from the surviving material the great number of variations in each motif and in the general composition and mood can be traced, and one of the aims of this book is to show the creative process through which Sutherland reached his final result, starting from a prescribed pattern on which he superimposed his own vision. The process through which this was achieved was so complex, there were so many influences at work and so many problems to be solved, that I felt that the authentic interpretation of the tapestry's genesis could only be given by the artist himself. This is why it was decided to present the main text of this book in the form of statements made by Graham Sutherland in reply to questions which I put to him.

A.R.

THE SUBJECT

AR: I understand that when you started to work on the first sketch, the iconographical details were laid down by the architect and the ecclesiastical authority. Therefore you had accepted a more or less clear-cut pattern, but one which you felt you could interpret in your own individual way?

GS: I hoped I could.

AR: Now one traditional representation of Christ in Majesty shows Him seated with the book with seven seals in His right hand and His left hand raised in blessing. Another shows Christ in Glory at the Last Judgment; here He does not hold the book, but either unfolds His hands or holds them upraised. I have been wondering whether your conception was a kind of synthesis of these two interpretations.

GS: I don't think I was really very conscious of either of your examples, except in this sense: for me the actual title—"Christ in Glory in the Tetramorph"—was the important thing. I do feel, on looking back (indeed I remember well what I felt at the time), that I wanted to create a figure of great *contained* vitality. All kinds of things came into my mind: references to parts of the Mass, for instance, where the priest, in order to emphasise the power contained in the Host, holds his hands in a certain position, parallel with the sides of the face and with the arms close to the body. My first conception of having a resigned Christ I abandoned. *Frontispiece* This was a Christ who was at once faintly accusing and resigned to the conduct of creation—of the human species in particular—and I changed my conception into something which I felt was perhaps closer to an idea of a scarcely contained spirit, a power. In fact, it was suggested to me at the time by the clergy that I should make Christ in a position of blessing. For me this was too hackneyed a pose, dusty with too long worship for such a figure as I envisaged. I felt that it must contain, together with the humanity of Christ, a sense of the *power* of Christ, in so far as Christ is also God. I did not want a Jehovah by any means, but on the other hand I wanted the look of the figure at least to have in its lineaments something of the power of lightning and thunder, of rocks, of the mystery of creation generally—a being who could have caused these things, not only just a specially wise human figure. My idea, then, was to make a figure which was a presence. And to surround that figure with the traditional layout of the four symbols of the Evangelists. In spite of suggestions that I do so, I did not attempt to interpret the letter of the Book of Revelation because I thought it was far too complicated and would lead me into labyrinths which were far too diffuse. I felt that what mysticism I had the power to express could be contained by very simple means through the traditional layout which became current in Romanesque art. But within such a framework I needed something different, the same and yet not the same. I needed to make the effect more immediate and a little bit more in line perhaps with my thinking of to-day—a claim I wouldn't like to suggest I have achieved. But those were the kind of thoughts that were passing through my mind. I also knew that this was not a subject with which I would have been ordinarily in sympathy. I didn't even know that I could do this subject. I knew of and had seen a good deal of past art, but I started consciously to look at a great deal more. I wanted to create a figure which was at once decorative and hieratic and at the same time a figure which really was a palpable presence. I didn't feel that there was any halfway house between doing a figure which was a symbol and doing something real. I felt that I must try for something which was as real as I could make it. Real in the sense that I always feel Egyptian figures are. I've told you that I went often to the Louvre and looked at the Egyptian figures. There is an art which is nothing if not aesthetic, that is to say the forms are subject to rigorous simplification and stylisation, but at the same time through this comes a feeling for reality. In the Egyptian rooms at the Louvre you feel faced by real people. I wanted something of that element. Curiously enough, I did not find this quality nearly so much in Christian art, except in those Pantocrator half-figures of Christ in the Byzantine tradition such as one sees in Greek churches.

AR: Indeed, representations of Christ which have in my view some affinity with yours are the works done under Norman rule in Sicily—those based on the Byzantine prototype but with a northern approach, such as one finds in Cefalù and Palermo. And being in the main mosaics, these are essentially two-dimensional. With the limitations of your medium, of tapestry, you must have had similar considerations: that is, your task wasn't, I think, one of creating space.

GS: I wanted to create a limited space—a space which was no deeper than you would find in a box. You may have noticed the lines suggesting a room which go behind the boxes from which the beasts appear and the bands of brass—I think of them as being brass. A propos of these, the bands of tape which bind the early Egyptian and Graeco-Roman portraits—burial bands which bound them to the coffins—fascinated me. I had a feeling that this would be a way to get away from the ordinary mandorla, which had for me too great an eccelesiastical flavour. You will notice, too, that the bands are more or less continuous and that they bind in the boxes containing the beasts and flow into them. Without stressing the symbolic aspect, I felt they also bound the beasts to the central figure. Whether to use a mandorla or not was a point which exercised me a good deal. It was calculated to lessen the sort of impact I wanted; it had been used far too much. But I felt that in some sense it would justify itself. It was a strong form, and I set about trying to find means of making it look valid, to make it look different. Of course in some drawings, particularly the early ones, the mandorla is used in a perfectly conventional way. In my first drafts I was accepting quite literally the sort of thing which I had seen in Romanesque art. Most of the sketches have got it in some form or other. Some of them, however, haven't, as for instance the second design, the one which I showed to the Reconstruction Committee. But I returned to the original design with the mandorla, although they had accepted this one, because I thought it had more power.

Plate 6

AR: I also feel that the face of the second design wouldn't have been as dominant as in the final version.

GS: No, possibly not. I think, too, that in this version the lacing of these boxes containing the beasts would have been more difficult to bind to the central figure.

All this time I was thinking that the figure must be at once remote and yet using gestures of to-day: by someone like the Pope, for instance. I am sure that in some sketches I was influenced by photographs of the Pope on the balcony of St. Peter's.

Plate 2

AR: This is, of course, the traditional way of blessing which already appears on tenth-century ivories depicting the priest celebrating Mass.

GS: Exactly. It's a gathering together, a sort of concentration more than a gesture; a sort of concentration of a spiritual force, a kind of holding of it, as it were. But though I studied this particular pose I didn't feel it was sufficiently remote.

AR: It's too human, perhaps.

GS: Let us say not sufficiently remote. I wanted the whole figure to be more taut. Then I tried all sorts of positions. I made a whole notebook of traditional gestures, of which you have seen examples. By doing this, I thought I would at least see what the gestures looked like and what had been done, and what use I could make of them—whether elements could even be interpreted into a new vocabulary of gestures; but I didn't find they could. It may sound immodest, but I became very critical of most of the old poses. I became full of admiration for the general impact of many of these early things, but I found so often that there was one element or another which the artist had not been able to solve. A single dominant figure is a very testing thing to do because it either becomes too symmetrical or it does not become symmetrical enough. And in a subject of this sort there were all kinds of overtones that I wished to try to avoid. I was more or less re-using something of the old pose which can so very easily look false. I did make one or two drawings of half-natural objects, that is to say leaves and parts of trees, which I felt might be of use. One of them, which was based on a piece of natural organic growth, I used as a sort of

Plate 12

Plate 10

parallel and a basis of the proportion for the figure. The figure is a series of ovals, separated by squares culminating in the head. This is the reason why the skirt has its particular shape in the final version, repeating the shape of the head. But that is not the only reason, of course. There were others. I wanted the figure to be real, yet not real. I wanted it to be something slightly ambiguous: a human form, but with overtones of a nature form. This posed the question of clothes.

AR: Did you have any instructions about the clothing of Christ or was this left entirely to you?

GS: It was left to me. In some of my earlier drawings the clothes were like winding-sheets. It would have been interesting to try and solve the problem along those lines, because I would have liked the clothes to be as mysterious and as ambiguous as possible. But after making several studies I decided to abandon that idea and to make the clothing more comprehensible and less complex in character.

Plate 15

AR: And the final solution is almost a priest's vestments.

GS: Yes. My idea was that it should be very close on the material side to a priest's vestment with a small abbreviated cape over the top. I tried to steer the delicate path between something which is actually worn and something which is conceptual, and I experimented with the large cape such as is worn by cardinals. It is an interesting shape, but I felt that in using it I was becoming too factual. Finally I used the small cape; it enabled me to show the arms separated and more forcefully, I think.

AR: Now another question in connection with the iconography: the representation of the Holy Ghost. Was it at the patrons' request or was it your wish to include it in the composition?

GS: It was suggested, as far as I can remember, by word of mouth. I thought that an opening at the top would look well. I remember when I was young seeing pigeons released through a hole high in a church wall at Easter. It would give a certain element of space, I thought. The green ground was a wall yet not a wall. Nearly everything in the design is in a sense ambiguous. Reading the background as a wall, it seemed not a bad idea to make an opening in the wall through which, far beyond the opening, there might be something visible.

AR: Am I right in assuming that the Holy Ghost didn't figure in the first sketches?

GS: At the beginning it figures. Then it disappears or it comes in a different form. It certainly doesn't appear at all in some drawings. But in most of them it does in some shape or other.

AR: Between the feet of Christ you represent Man, and it has often been stated that this figure is life-size and thus gives some idea of the scale of the whole tapestry. Now this is not a traditional symbol in Christian art.

GS: No. Not as far as Christian art is concerned.

AR: Could you tell me how this new motif was introduced by you—whether as a symbol of the measure of Man or as an indication of the scale of the work?

GS: The reason was mainly an aesthetic one. In looking at Egyptian sculpture I had seen often a figure between the feet of a god and the feeling it gave me was enormously moving. In my case, it was only too easy to rationalise its use into the idea of this being the measure of Man. When you appear in front of a committee of ecclesiastics and you are asked why you do certain things, the temptation to find a logical reason and to explain it in ecclesiastical rather than aesthetic language is overwhelming. The real reason was twofold: to give a sense of scale, and because I liked the look of it and the potency it seemed to give. Anything which adds a feeling of mystery in a work of this kind, any straw which one can grasp to heighten the sort of contained drama one is trying to get, is good. One could and should use anything which comes to hand and mind.

AR: Now, as far as I can see, the most drastic changes in the subject-matter took place in the sketches for the lower panel, where you experimented with a number of solutions. Could you give some indication of these changes: how far were they determined by iconographical and how far by aesthetic considerations? In your first sketch you had the Crucifixion in the lower panel and this is obviously a subject which is very close to you. Then, in the first full-scale cartoon, you had a Deposition or Pietà in the centre of the lower panel. Subsequently, at the request of your patrons, you devised for the lower part a triptych with three panels showing scenes from the life of the Virgin. Then again, this was abandoned and you reverted to the Crucifixion.

GS: As far as I can remember (it is difficult now to remember exactly), the idea was originally that the tapestry would not go right to the floor. There was under review the idea of having a series of windows beneath it going right across the end of the Lady Chapel. Alternatively, if the tapestry was to come right to the ground, then (an idea which was very close to the wishes of the authorities) the Twelve Apostles might appear at the bottom.

AR: No doubt as an illustration of St. Matthew's reference to the Last Judgment: "Ye which have followed me, in the regeneration when the Son of man shall sit in the throne of his glory, ye also shall sit upon twelve thrones, judging the twelve tribes of Israel" (Chapter XIX, verse 28). This motif occurs in a large number of Romanesque sculptural representations, as for instance at Bourges, Arles, Angoulême, and also Chartres.

GS: That's right. But I myself never liked this idea. For me, again, it had the seeds of disaster through being so hackneyed. From my point of view, it could so easily become to-day a conventional piece of ecclesiasticism.

AR: And although it also appears in Romanesque wall paintings, it's a perhaps more sculptural than pictorial concept?

GS: Possibly. In my view, it's not right for to-day. I then had an idea of having something in a central panel. There had been a lot of talk at that time of incorporating St. Michael and the Hosts of Heaven, and presumably the lost. Possibly a sort of Last Judgment. I considered the idea of having a lot of figures in the area (which is now blank) on either side of a central panel. That was my first idea of all and, in fact, I did quite a number of drawings of groups of figures rising and descending, rather along the lines of a Last Judgment. These don't exist any longer and it seemed to me, moreover, to make the thing very much too complicated. You must realise that during the whole time I had models of the Cathedral. I knew more or less what it was going to be like, although great changes were made in details. There were times when its design was more, or less, complicated; but its final form became eventually comparatively simple. I felt accordingly that a very complicated base was not going to give the impact that I wanted to the central figure and therefore I abandoned it.

The next stage was that I would have a series of panels at the bottom—the centre panel containing a Deposition, for which I made a number of sketches. The authorities always considered that what I called the retro-choir was a Lady Chapel, and therefore

Plates 66 & 67

they suggested some reference to the Madonna. I wanted what I thought should be a tragic element in the life of Christ in contrast to the risen Christ above; and therefore it came into my mind fairly early on that there should be a Pietà because I thought that this would embrace the two themes. It would be appropriate for a Lady Chapel and at the same time a good solution in relation to the figure above. So I designed a Pietà, and, in one of the early meetings in 1953 when the Bishop, the Provost and the Chairman of the Reconstruction Committee came down to my house, they all saw it and the Provost was strongly against having a Pietà. He suggested three panels representing scenes from the life of Christ, and that one of them should be a Madonna and Child. I did try out this idea; the central panel contained a Madonna and the two side panels the Visitation and the Annunciation. The second large version originally had these panels; it is now altered and contains a central panel of the Crucifixion, though the triptych still appears in a number of sketches. I didn't like the look of this solution with the three panels at all, and I never worked them out very far. Having decided that they wouldn't do, I put forward an alternative suggestion, with which I had flirted vaguely at the beginning, of having a Crucifixion in the middle. A lot of the early sketches half suggest a Crucifixion in this place; some of them half suggest, hardly a Deposition, but a sort of Pietà in which the Christ figure is more important than the subsidiary figures. When my new suggestion of a central Crucifixion was accepted, I went on with that.

Plates 68 & 69

Plates 70, 71 & 72

Plates 5 & 6

Plate 4

At this time there was the question as to whether there was going to be an actual reredos behind the High Altar—I mean a physical paling of some kind, possibly with the Twelve Apostles incorporated symbolically or otherwise, something semi-transparent in the sense that it would have spaces between, through which you could see the lower part of my tapestry behind it. When it was decided that there should be no reredos I thought that my single panel was going to prove more satisfactory both in relation to the rest of my theme and also to enable me to strengthen the bottom by having yellow bars behind it. These linked up with the sides of the chapel, thus correcting its tendency to narrowness. And there is this further point: at the time of the idea of a semi-transparent reredos it would not have been possible to consciously see my Crucifixion panel at all. The square of my panel would have been exactly covered. My conception at that time therefore finished visually at the foot of the mandorla, or just below it. When it was decided to do away with the reredos, the proportions I had originally intended became altered, in so far as one could now see *part* of the panel. In any case, the top of the high altar came higher than I had anticipated; therefore what would have been a complete screen or blocking of the area of my Crucifixion panel continued as a half-blocking. The 'weight' of the area of the proposed reredos as part of my design was therefore partially lost and, in my opinion, the base of the tapestry is now insufficiently weighted, certainly from near the altar.

AR: But to continue with the iconography, did the chalice with the dragon figure in the initial composition? *Col. Plate IX*

GS: No, this was a later addition. I don't think you will find it in the very early sketches.

AR: Was this yours or the patrons' initiative?

GS: It was my initiative.

AR: And did you introduce it for compositional or symbolic reasons?

GS: It is difficult to say, to analyse one's thinking of so long ago. I wanted a complex of interest below the feet.

AR: The chalice with the dragon often appears as a symbol of St. John the Evangelist, for instance in paintings by El Greco and Zurbaran. This is sometimes interpreted with reference to the Last Supper, connected with the legend according to which St. John was handed a cup of poisoned wine out of which, at his blessing, the poison rose in the shape of a serpent. You yourself also told me of another legend which has it that the Devil attempted to drink from the cup and was only saved from consequent death by the intervention of St. John. The chalice, of course, also represents the Precious Blood and, in his book,* Spence quotes the passage from Chapter XII, verses 3–11, of Revelation as referring to your motif: "And there appeared another wonder in heaven; and behold a great red dragon . . . Michael and his angels fought against the dragon. . . . And they overcame him by the blood of the Lamb." This brings us to another iconographical motif, the small panel of St. Michael. *Col. Plate VIII*

GS: In various documents and letters it was stressed that this was to be the Cathedral Church of St. Michael. I am sure that at

* Basil Spence, *Phoenix at Coventry*, London, 1962.

some time or another somebody said: "Don't you think you could put in St. Michael?" So I decided to introduce the motif and it is of course a useful element by which to gain a slight asymmetry in an otherwise rather symmetrical design.

AR: Reverting to the beginnings of the whole conception, it would appear that some of the first sketches were endeavours on your part to find the right scale in accordance with Spence's specifications.

Plates 1 & 3

GS: I was receiving at that time a number of architectural drawings from Spence himself. These incorporated his conception of the form which the tapestry might take. No doubt that he had the intention of giving me some idea of the weight and dominance of the central figure as he envisaged it in relation to the architectural plan.

His central figure, as I remember it, was in a mandorla and the components of the several drawings which he sent me varied somewhat in scale, in order to conform to the changes which at this time he was making in his design. I myself knew that, given the theme and with the proposed dimension in mind, I must make a large figure. But naturally, at this moment, I was afraid of being preconditioned—of being nudged into doing something which I might not want. I was anxious to be able to approach the subject freshly and in my own way.

AR: We have already referred to the two basic interpretations of Christ in Glory. The original one, based on the passage in Revelation in which St. John sees Christ surrounded by the four beasts, was traditional from the fourth or fifth century, lasting down to Romanesque and even early Gothic art, showing Christ with the book in His right hand. Of course, in Revelation the four beasts are not as yet associated with the Evangelists. Only later in early Christian literature were they linked up with the Gospels and remained their traditional emblems throughout the Middle Ages, though in fact they already appear in the visions of Ezekiel.

GS: The winged creatures with eyes inside and out?

AR: Yes.

GS: But the interesting thing, of course, is that as far as my knowledge goes no artist in any period, with the possible exception of William Blake, has taken the Book of Revelation at all literally. All the others, as I see it, have introduced a simplified outline of the idea or departed from the description given in nearly every respect—the sea of glass, for instance. The scenes and events described have not been followed directly, but interpreted in a *limited* way only. So far as the major interpretations of this subject are concerned—I think I am right in saying this—Blake alone seems to have attempted the scene as St. John described it, with the eyes and the number of wings—beasts yet not beasts. I know of no other example in Christian art where St. John's description is followed so exactly. On the other hand, what I find interesting is that the variants of the Christ figure plus the symbols of the

Evangelists have hardly changed in Christian art for many centuries. Incidentally, what was the first presentation of that subject —Christ in Glory? It didn't have any surrounding animals at all? Was it just Christ alone?

AR: In the first representation of the Ascension of Christ, the Glory is supported by angels without the symbols of the Evangelists. The latter, however, do appear right from the beginning in all representations based on the apocalyptic vision of Christ in Majesty.

GS: I see—presumably derived from two things, one imagines. The description in Revelation and the idea which was then becoming current of associating beasts with the writers of the Gospels. Surely very little is known as to what part the symbols played or how they were conceived? Were these symbols which are associated with the writers of the Gospels to do with the idea of creation, with created things, linking the pith and core of the Gospels with the idea of creation, or not? I have a feeling that it must have been so. My own idea about these beasts is that they were symbols of created things and objects, men, animals.

AR: The objects created by God.

GS: Yes, also plants, everything.

AR: And this is why you combine the lion, for instance, with a plant?

GS: No, not consciously. I tried to give each animal its own character rather than associate it, as is traditional, with its role as an heraldic symbol. I had in my mind that each animal should have its own special character, that is to say, that if it were wild, its wildness should be demonstrated; that the calf should be calf-like, the man man-like and the eagle eagle-like. And to allow them to display their own personal vitality. Only through this demonstration of their nature do animals pay unconscious tribute to the power which created them; by their violence or their softness, their eagerness or their predatoriness—all those things.

THE STYLE

AR: You have already spoken of various sources of inspiration such as early Christian and Egyptian art. Now, as to the stylistic approach, did you look consciously for a certain kind of inspiration from any of these or did you try to free yourself from any previous patterns?

GS: It is very hard entirely to separate the iconographical considerations from stylistic ones. They react the one on the other. From the iconographical point of view, I looked at everything that I could and made a point of getting to know things which I had not known before. On the one hand, I was designing for a Christian *culte* with all the implications of the history of the Christian religion in art behind it. I was conscious of all the accepted ideas of how Christ gradually came to be presented pictorially, the good representations and the banal ones, and the reasons underlying them. On the other, I was supposed to be doing an imaginative work for to-day. My task was to make an impact which was at the same time a little outside or at least different from that which had been done. It is a most difficult thing to explain: I wanted to free myself from what had been done but, equally, to know what to free myself from, I had to look at it. I decided that if I could work within the framework, from an iconographical point of view, of what had been done, I would be more free to interpret stylistically the various elements. I would be like a kite on a string, I would be bound down to something concrete; then I could feel myself more free to interpret within the forms to which I had bound myself.

AR: As with every work of art, the tapestry evokes for me certain associations. My primary one, as I said before, has to do with its function: the tapestry has the same overwhelming impact on the worshippers as did the Byzantine representations of the Pantocrator. To cite a contrast, the effect is very different from that of Giotto's Last Judgment in Padua, where Christ is only one of the actors in a long narrative drama; the spectator reads the whole history of the Last Judgment scene by scene, and Christ's figure doesn't particularly hold the eye.

The other association I have is with the hieratic style of the representation of Christ. This hieratic style is essentially oriental and Byzantine; it also penetrated into Western art, as one sees in Ravenna or Sicily, whenever this came under Byzantine influence. And I sense this hieratic quality in your composition, with its frontal pose, its strong symmetry and a certain rectangular rigidity with the exception of the ovals of the mandorla, Christ's face and the lower part of His body.

Yet another of my associations is again with Byzantine art.

This is Christ's face—not in expression but as the type with the beard, because during such periods of Christian art in the west as were more or less free of oriental influences, for instance in the Catacomb paintings, the works of the Carolingian renaissance and those of the High Renaissance, Christ was depicted on the lines of a Greek god, as epitomised in the Last Judgment in the Sistine Chapel.

GS: I think the question of the beard is a difficult one. I gave some thought as to whether to have a bearded Christ or not. I thought on the whole that it should be. I was doing something in the framework of the traditional layout. Besides, many people wear beards to-day, I argued; and those differences of interpretation I would make could be made within the traditional framework. The idea of correspondences, that is to say in this case the use of a past framework in alliance with a present-day immediacy, fascinates me. There is a vital electric spark which bridges the gap between things as different yet the same as, for instance, those Pantocrator Christs of which we were talking and Rembrandt's Christ. I think that in the back of my mind I would have liked to demonstrate this kind of correspondence and to make a synthesis.

AR: Yet another association I have is with the Gothic elements in your composition. I mean Gothic as a reversion to a predominantly spiritual content and at the same time release from the subordination to architecture which was the criterion of Romanesque art, thus embodying a higher degree of realism.

GS: I must confess that consciously I had no thoughts about this. I was very aware that my work must relate closely to the architecture, whether or not it were subordinate to it. Taking this into account, therefore, you could argue that I was more minded of Byzantine than of Gothic. I did naturally look at Rheims and

Chartres, but not specially in this connection. Of course, some of the figures at Chartres are still entirely subordinated to architecture and are really pillars or built into pillars.

From my point of view your suggestion is too much of a digression. Every painter, if he has seen a good deal of ancient art, has a host of impressions. I have already said that I wanted to create something closely allied to the architectural conditions. If I could make a figure which contained in it some of the quality of pent-up force which I had felt in Egyptian sculpture, then I might come closer to achieving what I wanted, which was to make a figure which had the immediate qualities of a living person.

AR: If we simplify the stylistic question as an expression of the artist's aims, then one might say that in Byzantine art it is the spirit which predominates and the physical presence is of secondary importance, whereas in antique art and in later trends based upon it, such as Carolingian art and the High Renaissance, the spirit is subordinated to the physical beauty of the body. But in Gothic art both aspects are present, and that is why I mentioned it. Later on again, the spiritual element became stronger and so did the distortions, because naturalism is not really important if you want to make a very strong impact. And I feel that in your work, whilst creating a forceful spiritual impact, you had at the same time the intention of creating a human presence and in certain respects your approach was strictly naturalistic, as for instance in Christ's feet.

GS: That was done to create a shift of emphasis. I believe that one can legitimately incorporate elements representational and conceptual. Sometimes this shift of treatment can be very potent; such a contrast in style can give a great significance to the parts and to the whole. To quote only one example, Picasso's sculpture 'The Goat': though more or less naturalistic, it is *very* realistic only in the treatment of the udder and underlines the essential smoothness and softness of this in contrast to the rest of the work, thereby achieving great significance. In my work for Coventry, I believe that the contrasts I made are perhaps not stressed *enough*. I could have rung the changes along these lines even more, possibly making only the head naturalistic.

AR: Is it not arguable that the whole might have suffered?

GS: There could have been a loss of unity, but, properly handled, there might have been a gain.

AR: To recapitulate, then, should I be right in saying that, to start with, you built up a vocabulary based on the traditional canonic representations of the past and then, as you worked on it, gradually eliminated such traditional gestures or motifs, replacing them by solutions which in your view correspond to contemporary concepts?

GS: Well, I think the matter really divides itself into three sections, the first being that, whatever the final outcome, I intended to use the traditional representation as a starting point. The second was that, although I did make a number of drawings of various poses and gestures from the past, I had no intention of using them: I merely wanted to know what had been done over a wide range. I did think it might be possible, although I never considered this very seriously, to utilise in some new way some of the poses I had already seen, but, apart from non-Christian art, I didn't find anything which really seemed to satisfy my inner sense of what the pose should be. Thirdly, I had a fairly clear conviction that it must be a frontal, though not necessarily totally symmetrical, pose; an asymmetrical one, however intriguing, wouldn't give that stillness which I wanted to get. Apart from the fact that I wanted the figure to be real-looking, a presence, I don't think I thought very much of contemporariness or otherwise. But the feeling of a paraphrase or reconstitution of the stillness one sees in some of the Pantocrator heads or busts I did want to get, and by slowly eliminating what I couldn't do I began to know what I could. That's really what it amounted to.

AR: Of course, the symmetrical representation is really peculiar to Byzantine art, and thence penetrated later into Romanesque representations.

GS: But on the other hand at least half of the Romanesque Christs are not symmetrical. They may sometimes be in the top half, but when it comes to the lower part, the skirt and feet are generally not so. One wonders sometimes how they hold together; and I believe they are most successful in mosaic or sculpture and least so when in paint. For some reason the medium of sculpture or mosaic seems to support a greater lack of symmetry than paint. I may be wrong, though; this is merely a theory of mine. At all events, I think this question of symmetry is a tremendously interesting psychological one. But the question of a need for symmetry or otherwise is very personal and is probably bound up with one's own physical needs; for example, one person lies in bed symmetrically and another doesn't. At various times in one's life, one's need for the one or the other changes.

AR: This symmetry is particularly marked in the feet. You did say that you made drawings from nature for the feet, using your own feet as a model in a mirror; and that you also did the same for the hands. Did you make studies from nature for the seated figure too?

GS: Yes, I did—quite a number of them. I also made a small

clay figure which I draped with pieces of rag. There are a number of drawings of this kind of thing. I tried to make the folds over the small figure as simple as possible; I wanted to see how they fell. Of course they did give me a certain amount of information when it came to the final work.

Plates 17 & 18

AR: Does the clay figure still exist?

GS: No.

AR: Now the position of Christ underwent quite a considerable transformation between the initial sketches and the final tapestry.

GS: Yes, I must have done a great number of drawings of all kinds, but forming two main groups. First, my notes of existing figures in ancient art; secondly, a sort of new vocabulary of possible solutions of my own conception based on drawings made from this clay figure. I tried a number of different solutions for the drapery. Using this method is a gamble. To put drapery over a lay figure and hope that the folds are going to be those which you can use is entirely a question of luck. One may spend hours and hours changing the direction of the folds; suddenly these may just fall so that they look absolutely right. Then the difficulty is keeping it wet enough to stay in that position. I think it is much easier probably on a larger figure than on a very small one. There is little room to manoeuvre with the latter and it is a very delicate task. But I believe that, in the same way as by constant observation of nature the lucky chance falls into one's lap, so in using a model in this way one may be able to produce a much more mysterious realism, using the forms as they actually happen and interpreting them, rather than inventing them.

Plate 14

Plate 11

AR: You mean translating nature.

GS: Translating the thing that actually happens, in fact.

AR: This seems to me the same principle as you follow in your landscape painting.

GS: Very much the same. The final arrangement of the drapery was also governed by the position of the arms. I offered the Committee two alternatives, and they had to decide whether they preferred the arms raised or in the downward position. I confess I argued in the direction of not having them down, because at that time I thought it was more sentimental. I think that there is some gain in having the arms down from the point of view of composition: it gives a certain strength and linear relationship with the outside panels. To sacrifice the arms in the downward position gave me a great deal of difficulty in knowing how to fill the spaces on either side of the waist. This I did eventually by enlarging the base of the sleeves. *Plate 27*

AR: In one sketch the draperies have an almost oriental look. *Plate 13*

GS: Yes. I suppose it was one of the attempts which I made to escape from the conventional silhouette of quasi-Roman or Gothic draperies. Sometimes the priest's cape has a border of fur which comes down like a T-piece; it goes round the neck and hangs straight down in front. This again I thought might give the figure a certain difference and strength. One is always looking for means to give works of this kind a certain structural and decorative strength. *Plate 8*

AR: I notice that there is still a certain difference, even between the final cartoon and the tapestry itself, because the horizontal lines of the drapery are more emphasised in the cartoon; thus the oval shape is more marked in the tapestry. *Plate 9* *Col. Plate I*

GS: The area which is filled—the white area from the sash down, for which I made a supplementary cartoon—is in fact almost identical in both so far as the outside contour is concerned.

The difference lies in what goes on inside it. The corresponding area in the final cartoon only appears more horizontal by the fact of my having sacrificed certain folds, especially at the bottom, during the actual weaving of the tapestry. The skirt in the tapestry, it is true, appears more vase-like and therefore less horizontal, but the area is the same.

AR: Now I would like to take this up, because when we went to Coventry together we asked people their views and, you remember, they criticised the fact that they couldn't tell whether Christ was seated or standing, although in the cartoon He is quite clearly seated. By removing some of the horizontal folds a floating impression is created. Did you do this on purpose, in order to have a more spiritual presence, or was it for purely compositional reasons?

GS: I think neither. The main reason was that I felt that this shape in the final maquette before the weaving wasn't very satisfactory. It was too similar in shape to the space from the knees upwards, and too much of a repetition of the upper part. I also wanted to make the form a little more rhythmic. I wasn't very concerned about the ambiguity as to whether the figure was seated or standing. I didn't want to make it specifically sitting; in fact, I didn't mind a hint of ambiguity. It is difficult and basically absurd to try to give reasons for the unconscious impulses of one's mind. At the time when I made these final changes I was attempting to keep up with the progress of the weavers, for they had a time limit. What I might have done if there had been more time I don't know. I might have introduced certain lines inside this big area, rather more strong, if I had been given time. There is another factor from the weaving point of view: in full scale the skirt is a very big area, over twenty feet in height; I thought there wasn't enough in the final cartoon for the weavers to get hold of and interpret, and that was one reason why I tried to rationalise that part. I myself think the alteration was a gain, but I also think that in order to gain some things you lose others. As I have said, I believe the proportion of the oval to the rest of the figure is what I wanted and, as you can see from that early leaf-form drawing, it is strongly in line with what I had been aiming at from the beginning. *Plate 10*

AR: Now I would like to ask a few questions about the stylistic evolution of the four emblems. My impression is that the process of evolution in the cases of the eagle and lion is not unlike that of Picasso's fourteen portraits of Sylvette. His first version was an entirely realistic likeness which he subsequently stylised and distorted. Similarly, you started with perfectly straightforward, realistic studies of eagles and lions.

GS: I made drawings at Maidstone Zoo and Museum; also from photographs in magazines. *Plates 43, 48 & 49*

AR: Also one of the lion studies seems to me in line with the traditional representation of the St. Mark emblem of Venice, and in fact shows a suggestion of mosaic. *Plate 42*

GS: Yes, it was done at a time when I'd been in Venice. I also did a free copy of one of the lions in St. Apollinare in Classe just outside Ravenna. *Plate 44*

AR: I also feel that, more than any other parts of the tapestry, these four emblems convey the imaginative, fantastic quality of Romanesque art. Now the number of sketches for each emblem varies; there are a great many for the Eagle, less for the Lion and Man, and only four for the Calf. Does this mean your conception came more easily for some than for others?

GS: The two panels which gave me most difficulty were the top ones—the Man and the Eagle. The reason I did so many studies for the Eagle was because I couldn't get what I felt to be a really satisfactory form to fit into the given shape. I drew some flying, with wings folded round the head, others more hieratic in treatment. I was trying to do two things: to get away from an heraldic feeling and to give a certain strangeness and potency to the actual bird. Eagles are not normally birds that specially attract me; nor, among animals, are lions. Their image is rendered too dusty by tradition and by their heraldic connotations.

Plates 46, 47, 51 & 54

AR: But aren't you attracted by the expression of birds of prey?

G.S: Yes. Nonetheless, the eagle and lion have to be taken out of their glass cases; but the eagle's near cousin, the eagle owl—that kind of bird I love. On the other hand, the heraldic connotations appal me. I was trying always to put my eagle into a position of reality. I finally decided that I could perhaps do best by making the bird as if it had alighted.

Plate 52

AR: But you also did a very stylised, Sphinx-like one. *Plate 50*

GS: Yes. I was even going to give it breasts. It's not in relation to the other studies, really; it's quite on its own. Subsequently I settled on a variant both tonally and stylistically of the same weight and sort of expression which I had used for the Lion and Calf. I decided that the pose must be fairly static and that I must get all the expression of character, as unheraldic in the circumstances as possible, in the head itself; I was interested here simply in the construction of the beak and the eyes, and in rendering these in a clear, cogent way. *Plate 54 & Col. Plate VI*

AR: If one compares your first with your final cartoon, one can see that you changed your original concepts for the Eagle and Man very substantially, whereas the Calf and Lion remain much the same. Were there reasons for this? *Frontispiece and Plate 9*

GS: It is difficult to explain why one abandons a certain motif: I would have been perfectly prepared to develop my first cartoon further. The danger, of course, of working a long time on something is that one gets bored with what one has done and, out of relief more than anything else, one makes a change. Similarly I altered the Man.

AR: It's rather Egyptian in the first cartoon, isn't it?

GS: Possibly. One of my biggest difficulties was this emblem of the Man; I couldn't imagine what form it should take. It may be easy enough to arrange a male figure in various positions, but what sort of a figure was one to make for this man with wings? I didn't especially *want* a man with wings. What was he supposed to be doing? Worshipping God? But how? Above all I wanted to avoid the usual clichés and also any sort of sentimentalism or overformalised pose. Even in Egyptian art which I admire, in works where figures are supplicating the sun, there tends to be an over-formality about the position of the hands which for me can become far too much like a motor-car mascot. It seemed to me that one could only avoid this by thinking how people move their hands when they are entranced by some spectacle. The pose in this first cartoon is far too elementary.

There is no doubt that certain gestures—a vocabulary of gestures—cannot be used to-day: I noticed a photograph in the paper the other morning of a Last Judgment by some contemporary artist. All the gestures were Renaissance gestures and these just didn't work. One should of course make a new vocabulary (I have often thought of doing this in general, not in relation to any specific commission) not only of gestures which people use in ordinary life but also of religious gestures. People do clasp their hands in church, but they do a number of other curious things as well, and one feels one ought to be able to find something valid for to-day. To me, the version in question hadn't got it at all, and that's why it was abandoned. And so, eventually, the idea gradually evolved on the cartoon itself—the idea that it should be a figure expressing the eagerness of man—coming out of a window. I wanted to try and express a certain tense eagerness.

Plates 35–38 Col. Plate V

AR: There's a great deal of tension and movement in the subsequent sketches and final result, whereas its counterpart, the Eagle, has become more static.

GS: I tried to give each figure as much as I could its natural character: the predatory quality of the eagle, the ferociousness of the lion, the calm bovine quality of the calf, slightly hysterical, very easily afraid, and in addition the eagerness of the man, without any kind of overtone.

AR: But the conception is of Man worshipping God?

GS: Yes. Eager to understand, eager to feel, eager to see.

AR: The Lion, of course, changed much less between the first and final versions.

GS: Yes. I thought that such change as there was gave a certain stability in this corner which I felt it needed, particularly since, after all, the tune finishes there. If one can allow the analogy of music, this starts with the Calf and goes clockwise round the area. The form the Lion took, both in itself and in so far as its box is concerned seemed to me to describe the end of the tune.

Col. Plate VII

AR: As far as I can see, the Calf underwent hardly any change at all. Throughout the various sketches it appears the most consistent motif.

GS: Having fairly early on got at a comparatively satisfactory relation between this image in its panel and the rest of the work, I

Plates 39–41

didn't feel it necessary to alter it very much. Its working out came fairly naturally although, had I had time, I would have liked to have tried quite different interpretations.

Col. Plate IV

AR: In the light of what you say, I have the feeling that there were two processes: in one way you simplified your original conceptions, and in another you made them more involved and complex.

GS: Yes, I think that's true.

AR: In some of the first sketches, the composition was very complicated and rather rich, with definitely baroque qualities. Even in the last but one version you had Christ with the robe opening in the middle which was far more complex than the final version. On the other hand I find the emblems gradually became more and more intricate both in relation to the whole composition and also in their individual significance. What you have just been saying seems to confirm this.

Plate 8

GS: Yes, you're perfectly right. Of course there was a physical reason. Once having decided to make the basic composition simple, one then had to think of what it was going to look like on this very big scale. Also the composition was a centrifugal one. Therefore I thought that the outer points of interest could afford to be fairly complicated, and that was why I made them as I did. Had they been much more simple there would have been emptiness. With a work half the size one could have afforded a great deal more simplification, and that applies also to the actual texture of the background. This was another point that exercised me. What would happen to those very big spaces of green when the tapestry was in its full scale, unless the green was broken up in some way? I decided that there should not be a completely flat colour: it must be broken.

AR: I also noticed an interesting evolution in your concept of the Crucifixion. You have an early drawing which is a purely spiritualised version with the extremely strong, exaggerated Gothic swing; and then, in the final execution, you became much more realistic. So in this case it was another process, from a strongly spiritual representation to more realistic ones.

Plates 58 & 63
Col. Plate X
Plates 62, 64 & 65

GS: When you say realistic, do you mean to say that the later pose is a more possible one? It is certainly a less romantic one. I was concerned in the Crucifixion, I think, without doubt with two things. One, that in my final version there was going to be only one figure, that is to say there were not going to be the mourning figures at either side. I liked the idea that people in the Cathedral looking at the work are the mourners. But in abandoning the ancillary figures I was forced to abandon a figure on the Cross in movement. It is possible if one uses a number of other figures in relation to a curvilinear figure, in which the various movements are interlocked, to achieve a stable, counterbalanced design. A single figure in movement, I felt, would be too disturbing to the near-symmetrical, overall design. If I'd had a chance or time to experiment a great deal further with various less familiar poses, which have incidentally been in my mind for a number of years, I would have

welcomed it; but to use these suddenly in the context of the rest of the tapestry would have been, I feel, wrong. You will have noticed, in addition, another point: the Crucifixion panel is more finished than the rest. This is because it is meant to be seen close to, from within ten feet or so, in the Lady Chapel.

AR: Talking again about the Crucifixion, I was rather taken with the sun and moon, which look like two flowers. It interested me that you should have carried over the ambiguity one always finds between organic and inorganic elements in your landscapes into a representation which is normally rather canonic and conventional.

But turning now to the main figure of Christ, did you make any actual studies for His head from nature?

GS: No. I made studies from nature for the figure only. I studied the proportions of my own head, and I looked at myself in a glass with regard to lighting and so on. The final head really derived from a hundred different things—photographs of cyclists, close-ups of people, photographs of eyes, Egyptian art, Rembrandt and many others.

Col. Plates II & III

AR: And perhaps El Greco?

GS: Not El Greco at all.

AR: Yet to me there is a certain similarity, above all in the first cartoon, and that is one of the reasons why I think it is important to have this on record. Because I feel certain that, if other people write about it, they may well claim Greco associations which as you say are wrong.

Plate 24

GS: They are. I know exactly the genesis of the head. I can show you photographs in *Paris Match*, for instance, showing athletes—but they happened to be rather strange heads and you might think them a most unlikely source for this subject! Then there were the Rembrandts, and one wonderful, untypical Romanesque painting at Tavant (Touraine). This fresco at Tavant was, I would think, done from an actual person, or partly so: it has all the irregularities of a real head. The nose is not straight and the bridge is slightly bent, the moustache and beard are irregular.*

AR: One could call it realistic.

GS: Yes, but not naturalistic; it just looks authentic. It's a strange mixture of the two. It was this sort of inspiration which was of value. But I found the head really came *comparatively* easily. It differs little from the first cartoon onwards. As I progressed I tried to make it a little more electric in impact and I slightly altered the proportions, and the size and tone of the eyes. The head in the first version is also more sentimental than the final one and I was, it is true, conscious that it was over-sentimental and ought to be rather more human and stronger. But, you know, the look of a face can be so easily due to the tiniest difference in proportion or the slightest extra touch and this sometimes merely because one has put a spot of paint in the wrong place. It's as simple as that. One can make a face very sentimental or quite the reverse just by a touch.

Plates 24, 25 & Col. Plate III

AR: So you wouldn't say this was a change in your concept? It was more or less accidental?

GS: Accidental to the extent that I have described.

AR: Now we come to the hands.

GS: Most of the studies for the hands were done after the cartoon was finished. I think some must have been done in order to get the cartoon to a certain stage of finish, but then the problem came when the weavers sent me the photographic enlargements as soon as they had got to the stage of the arms and hands. At this

* *See* Focillon, *Peintures Romanes des Eglises de France,* Paris, 1938, Plate 74.

time, therefore, I started making a great number of studies from my own hands in a mirror until I arrived at one which I used finally with slight alterations in the actual length of the fingers, together with its reverse, so to speak.

Plates 28, 29, 30 & 31

AR: And this was done simultaneously with the weaving?

GS: Yes, when the photographic enlargements were sent to me at Menton, in 1961.

AR: And lastly, what about the feet? Did they raise any problems?

GS: I made some studies for the cartoons. They were badly drawn; even so, I was loath to alter them. Then, when I saw them enlarged on the photographs supplied by the weavers, I decided they must be redrawn. And I started to make a lot of new diagrams. The frontal view creates problems and to arrive at a shape which is both interesting and looking like a foot at all is not easy. I wanted this frontal view, however; it seemed an essential part of the whole thing. All these studies were various attempts to analyse the possibilities of a foot in that position. Most were done from my own feet in a mirror and are very incomplete. Finally I selected one as more or less the final version.

Plates 32 & 33

Plate 33

AR: And this very strong, realistic impact of the feet makes a certain contrast to the spiritual quality of the head. Was this done deliberately?

GS: No, not consciously so. The treatment of the feet was simply part of my desire to make a compact figure of *contained* power and with a completely frontal look. It is no good trying to read into my intentions symbolic or quasi-spiritual meanings. If a figure has any kind of spiritual power it is because it is felt as such. I did not say to myself: "Let us have clumsy feet so that we can make the head more spiritual." The feeling one has—if it is strong enough—generates its own technique which will express it. If the feeling is not strong, the technique will be weak. But there is always the fact that one has to find material to feed on; a vocabulary, in fact. One might as well ask a rose why it has its particular form. It would, if it could speak, tell you that it was its nature. But it might also tell you that its gardener had given it good manure.

AR: Is there anything else you would like to add about the stylistic elements?

GS: I think the only thing I could add is something of which you must be conscious yourself. This was to be a more or less symmetrical composition: at the same time I wanted to avoid total symmetry. Therefore the sizes and placing of the boxes were pretty carefully calculated and worked out to give some sort of overall balance. Total balance must be unbalanced; the mandorla is deliberately not symmetrical. It had to be very carefully adjusted to prevent the figure, which *is* as symmetrical as I could make it, from appearing *over*-symmetrical. There was a constant juggling with its lines, especially where they came near the figure.

THE MEDIUM

AR. Now I would like to know how far you were influenced by the medium for which you were working. Did you feel this a handicap or that in some ways it enhanced the possibilities, enabling you to express certain rather complex relationships which perhaps couldn't have been expressed in paint? I know you had a great deal of previous experience, and that designing for tapestry was by no means new for you.

GS: I think that the experience to which you refer was a factor which governed the method that I decided to use in the cartoon for this work, because I found it to be the case that by working my cartoon comparatively small, say a tenth of the intended final size, certain accidental qualities which result from the movement of a paintbrush, when translated into tapestry, don't look like paint but achieve a new dimension. But this happens only if the cartoon is enlarged; when it is blown up in a photograph, a change has already occurred. A touch becomes different when a thing is four times the size of the original.

AR: But isn't this true for any medium?

GS: Not necessarily. When a tapestry is finally woven from such a photograph, there's yet another change, and it was my experience that that change was a beneficial one. I don't specially work with the woven medium in mind; I am not a purist. But my technique does seem to translate into tapestry. The weavers themselves said that the work had a good tapestry quality, although they originally thought it wouldn't have. They were, so it seemed, anxious to "rationalise" the shapes that I made, that is to say, supposing a curve was infinitely variable along its contour, they would tend to make it simpler and so lose the character of the drawing. One of the things I had to guard against was this loss of the variety of contour—that black thread which goes through the whole thing and which I wanted preserved in all its complexity.

Tapestry weavers to-day are inclined to be trained to do only work which is likely to be flat with scarcely any variation of texture at all, or else have a very fine and infinitely graduated texture such as you see in a painting by Léger. That they can do marvellously, but I think they've lost a little owing to the fact that they have tried to make reproductions of abstract paintings with big, flat surfaces. Thereby I think they risk sacrificing a little of their skill. But, all things considered, I found their work for me and in general magnificent.

AR: It was probably very difficult for them to cope with the huge surfaces of the background, to ensure that it shouldn't be monotonous, yet see to it that it remained background.

GS: I think they didn't find so much difficulty with that. They probably found difficult the subtle changes of white—very large areas of white—in the robe. Perhaps I am right in thinking that they also found a certain amount of difficulty where two blacks were very close to one another in tone. The whole tapestry is really a sort of mosaic of tones and I took great care to explain that I wanted them to achieve graduations, not by the use of shading but by means of several patches of different tones. It is really the old Aubusson method; in those carpets every rose was built up in nuances of separate tones—ten pinks, for instance, to describe the form of one petal. Exactly the same technique has been used in this work of mine. The nuances are made by a lot of tones side by side rather than a merging of one tone into another. Some graduation is used, but very little.

AR: Did they have any difficulties with the face?

GS: The time element had become acute for them when they began this. On my last visit the head had been started and it seemed to be going very well. I asked if they anticipated any problems. No, I was told, it was likely to be the easiest part because it was more finished than the rest and very little in it was left to chance. All they had to do was copy the shapes of the tones. They knew that this area was the most exacting and that extra care had to be taken with it. One woman did the whole face.

AR: Did you, while working on your design, derive any conscious inspiration from other tapestries, either past or present?

GS: No, I don't think so.

AR: You didn't think, for instance, of the Angers tapestries of the Apocalypse, or of contemporary tapestries done after Picasso?

GS: I knew what the firm of Pinton could do. It was through my friendship with Madame Cuttoli, who is artistic director of Pinton's and who played such a part in the revival of tapestry in France, that I was able to make the firm known to the Coventry authorities and persuade them to use it. Originally, Spence's idea was that the Edinburgh tapestry company should do the work. This firm had a Mr. Cruickshank as head weaver, and I was quite glad about this because Cruickshank had in fact made one tapestry with which I was extremely pleased and has subsequently made another. He is a very good craftsman indeed. I went up to

Edinburgh to see a trial piece which he had done of the Calf. Given the restricted amount of time in which he had done this, it seemed to me to be fairly good. It has lost some of the drawing, however; even so, I had no real anxiety about this as I was sure that, given proper time, he would have done very well. Unfortunately, Cruickshank left the firm, which was taken over by a new management. They produced another trial piece, for which I had suggested a passage in the head, round the eye, as a good test. At this point it seemed that this particular firm would not be able to weave the tapestry on the looms available in one piece and, rather reluctantly, Sir Basil Spence and I thought that it would be preferable if this could be done. My mind then turned to Madame Cuttoli, whom I had known for some time. I wrote to her, asking if she would be prepared to undertake the work, and she replied that she would be very happy to do so. Accordingly, in consultation with Spence and the Reconstruction Committee, she was asked officially to undertake it. I knew that she was the best person in the world to do this work; moreover, I knew that the tapestry could be made at Pinton's in one piece.

I had, as a matter of fact, seen the tapestries they had done from cartoons by Picasso which Madame Cuttoli owns. This taught me rather a lot. The cartoons were not done specifically in a tapestry technique, but they turned out as I saw to be exceptionally true tapestries. With this example before me, it did not seem necessary to work strictly in a calculated tapestry technique. Provided that a good deal of scope is given for the weavers to interpret and unless one uses a very fluid technique such as free oil paint, a tapestry-like quality can follow through the process of interpretation.

I certainly didn't look at the great tapestries of the past. It's a medium which I find rather dead and cold, though this view doesn't apply to the Coptic fragments which I had seen. But I had never been very moved by the medium until I saw the tapestries done by Madame Cuttoli's factory at Algiers during the war. Strictly speaking, these were of course really copies of paintings, but they had such a beautiful texture and were full of vitality.

AR: Whose paintings were they done from?

GS: Braque, Rouault, Picasso, Léger, Miro. Although these paintings weren't specifically designed for tapestry, most of them eventually achieved the unmistakeable quality of tapestry. The marvellous set of two still lifes by Braque were not in the least like the paintings from which they were done. And technically they were every bit as good as some of the great tapestries of the past, with a wonderfully fine stitch. Somehow they had become tapestries. But by far the best were those done from Matisse and Picasso. On the whole, however, unlike many other interpretative mediums such as lithography, I find tapestry isn't something I really take to. Would I ever have done a cartoon for this work in tapestry if I had had the choice? On the other hand, how would one find the strength to cover in an area of that size through any other medium?

AR: Were you handicapped, during your work, by thinking that it would be translated into another medium?

GS: No. I went to a great deal of trouble to find out the size of the stitch and to get a sample piece done, so that I could see what effect the translation might have. My real preoccupations were not with what could be done, because I was pretty certain almost anything could be done, but with the effect of the enlargement.

AR: Another point I wanted to mention is the scale. When working on the cartoon, you had to keep in mind all the time how it would look in the final size when enlarged from a height of seventy-two inches to over seventy-two feet. I understand that the cartoon was enlarged photographically in panels. Did this induce you to make certain changes?

GS: I always had the intention of working on the actual photographic enlargement. This I did on every strip. The enlargement was divided into yard-high strips running the full width of the tapestry, about forty feet. There were twenty-two or three of these. I was able to pin them up on the wall of a disused shop which the Mayor lent me in Menton. It had been a big department store. At the most, I could pin up five at a time, but generally not more than four. And some I worked on in my own studio. There I could only have two up at a time. And I went over all the parts which I thought needed clarification. I outlined quite a number of forms sufficiently to give an indication of the kind of simplification that I wanted, showing what the weavers were to leave out. There

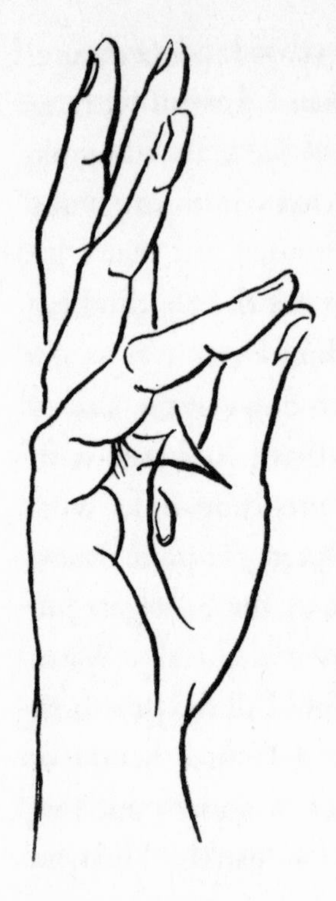

was a great deal that they *had* to leave out for technical reasons and certain things were a matter of choice. Those things which I wanted to retain I had to make clear. In addition, I did do a good deal of redrawing. This was necessary. In the original cartoon, for instance, the little Crucifixion at the bottom, not more than about a foot square, was too small in scale to enable me to draw the hands or feet of the figure on the Cross. So I redrew those on the photograph. I also redrew the Calf's head, the yucca tree in the Lion's compartment and, as you know, the whole of the skirt. Similarly, I did the whole of the feet—and the hands—again, in black and white on the photograph. A complication was that I had no colour to refer to; the weavers had the coloured cartoon and wanted to use it to work from. Eventually I went to Felletin and the weavers and I conferred as to methods of using the colour of the cartoon in relation to the corrected drawing I had done on the strips.

AR: What, in terms of time, were the principal stages from the date of the commission to the final completion?

GS: The work went in waves. At the beginning, while I concentrated on the design, I really couldn't manage much other work. I did some painting and certainly two portraits—Churchill and Sackville-West. In fact, the work for the tapestry divided itself, I suppose, into about three or four stages. One, doing innumerable drawings without very much purpose, to clear the ground. I was not certain at the beginning what kind of figure I wanted. I had a model of the Cathedral and in it I would arrange a miniature design now and again to see what the scale was going to be. Gradually variations of treatment came into my mind. Finally, towards the end of that longish period, I felt that I had got to make some kind of positive statement. I did the first cartoon. The figure itself was done fairly quickly. There was a good deal of alteration in the surrounding panels, but not very much in actual proportion. Up to this point everything had been continuous. Then there was quite a big gap of time because I wanted to look at what I had done and to consider it. The authorities wanted to see progress so far as it had gone. They made a preliminary visit to my house. I was told to go ahead. After that, I wasn't really sure whether I liked what I had done. During the January of '54 we were at Roquebrune and I started to do another version with the arms horizontal. I worked on that quite a bit and rather liked it. Then came another gap. Later I started to do a cartoon on the Roquebrune version. I took this to Coventry together with the original version which they had already seen, and appeared before the Committee at a first meeting. They made one or two suggestions. The idea seemed to be liked in principle. I showed it together with the previous cartoon and they preferred this second one. Then I didn't feel that either was the solution. When you're working on something for a long time, you tend through knowledge to get restless about it. I thought I could do better; so I started to prepare a third design. I again went to Coventry, taking this with me, and they passed it. As soon as I reached home, I knew that I heartily disliked the one that had been approved. I then started not to make another cartoon but to strip this third one of its inconsistencies and to redraw some of the

Frontispiece

Plate 6

Plate 7

Plate 8

panels—the St. Matthew panel, for instance, at the top left-hand corner. A great deal was done and the lower part of the central figure was entirely recast. All this had to be compressed into a pretty short time, because the authorities were anxious to get the weaving started. They were clamouring for a press release, so I had to work in a very concentrated manner and eventually reached the stage which formed the definitive cartoon. This was released, rather against my will, because I wanted to work at it more. But it went to the weavers. This was in 1958. I still pressed for more time, but agreed that the weavers could make a start on the Crucifixion panel at the bottom provided they would wait for me to re-draw the hands and feet on the blown-up photographs. This was the pattern of progress from then on. I, knowing full well what still had to be altered, decided that any rectifications which I wanted to make now must be made during the course of the weaving.

AR: How many years did the actual weaving take?

GS: I think over two and a half years.

AR: And during that time were you permanently preoccupied with the tapestry?

GS: Yes. From then on, apart from short bursts of other work which I took time off to do, I was preparing the material for the weavers to work on. I suppose I'm optimistic and think things are going to pan out, but the weavers got ahead of me. They used to send me terrible telegrams: "Must have strips 23, 24, 25, by Friday." These had to be packed and sent off by train. What was concerning me all this time was that I might still have the chance to recast certain parts which I wasn't satisfied with. And the corrections I made were, I think, of service to the whole.

AR: Did you spend quite a lot of time yourself at Aubusson?

GS: About two days every four months.

AR: And did they have to unpick certain parts on your instructions?

GS: They only went wrong on the sort of thing you might expect occasionally, because some people have a good eye for tone and others haven't. There were I think about twelve people in all working on the tapestry. Out of these, there were three principal weavers, whose task was concerned with the three obviously most difficult parts, that is the central figure and the panels, two on each side. A girl working on the left-hand panels might well have begun with a superiority in skill to her colleague working on the two right-hand panels; but during the long process of weaving, the degree of excellence in skill could change, and often did. Therefore I had occasionally to give instructions for small sections to be unpicked and done again. But it was difficult to know how much, because I only saw as much as was wrapped once round the roller at a time; the rest of course was hidden. The method is very primitive. The weavers are working from great experience, but even they are not able to see more than this at any one time and they cannot see the part in relation to the whole.

AR: Were the wools specially dyed for you?

GS: Yes. The colours were impeccable. I was very careful about this in any case: one of the very first things I did was to go through the colours with M. Pinton and his director.

AR: On the whole, you didn't change your images while you were redrawing them on the enlargements?

GS: A big photograph, however good, misses out certain details. The grain of the negative becomes too strong in certain areas and the effect becomes broken with spots. These had to be eliminated. The large photograph, moreover, emphasised little flicks of white or black which in the original are minute. How many of these should be incorporated? Should I take advantage of some of these little shapes—accidental in the cartoon? In certain cases I retained them; in others I eliminated them. In some areas I felt that the treatment was unsatisfactory when I saw it in the full scale, and these parts I redrew, sometimes even making new studies. Most of the time it was a question of reworking and clarifying. Sometimes a part would be so vague one could hardly see it and it had to be redelineated. The weavers would otherwise have had an impossible task. The photograph itself was not very good. This was a handicap.

Col. Plate IX

AR: I see that in the lower background for the Chalice they got a sort of moiré effect.

GS: That was from a piece of actual material pasted over the cartoon. I had an idea of using more stuck-on cloth in my design because I know how well it can be reproduced. It is also a fact that the addition of a material different from the medium in which a work is mainly done can give a new dimension and a shock of surprise—things such as using real cane in a painting of a cane chair, or sticking sacking on a painting. For the same reason I tried embroidered white moiré for the robe of Christ, and indeed on some of the panels I originally had a cloth background. Finally I retained it only for the background to the Chalice.

RELATION TO ARCHITECTURE

AR: I should like to ask you a few questions about the influence of the architectural surroundings. No doubt when Spence first visited you to discuss the whole project, he also outlined his conception of the building and you were subsequently provided with a working model of it.

GS: Yes, I was sent the plans and a scale working model very early. But the design, as you know, was altered several times, though not necessarily in those parts which affected me directly. During all the various changes Spence kept me closely informed.

May I digress now for a moment in order to stress circumstances in this connection. Spence, during the years following the start of the commission, could not have been more helpful. Not only did we discuss frankly and freely the various changes to his design which he was making, but he generously lent the weight of his authority, in full and understanding knowledge of my intentions, not only at the critical meetings of the Reconstruction Committee which I attended at Coventry, but also at my house on the occasions when he brought the various persons in authority there during the period when I was making the designs. This welcome co-operation seemed to evaporate during the last few months of the weaving and its loss clouded the days when I was in need of support in order to exercise my contractual rights and duties, which were to see if my design had been properly interpreted. This period of discord is now in the past, however, and there is no point in going into its various aspects here.

But I have digressed too much. We were talking about the alterations which were being made to the design of the cathedral itself and you were, I know, about to ask me a question relating to these changes.

AR: Yes, I wanted to ask you how far these alterations affected your work.

GS: In some ways they gave me more to do; in others they were a help.

AR: To begin with, I understand that the shape was altered.

GS: Yes, but that was very largely done at my own request. It was decided to make the proportions of the retro-choir narrower because it seemed clear to both Spence and myself that a narrower shape would be better both architecturally and for the proportions of the tapestry.

AR: And later there was also an alteration in the colour of the internal finish.

GS: We realised that the original idea of having the interior, but more especially the retro-choir, finished in red sandstone might very well make the whole area too dark. Given such colour close to my work in this chapel, I had visualised a series of dullish green tones, rather like old velvet; a muted scheme with the figures looming out of a comparatively dark ground. The only colour I would have permitted myself would have been in the panels. But then I thought that the retro-choir and indeed perhaps the whole cathedral might have tended to be too dark and, after talking it over with Spence, he decided that he would make the retro-choir lighter, mainly, I believe, so that I could introduce more colour. He later treated the whole of the nave in its present whitish colour.

AR: At what stage was the decision taken to make this chapel white? Was the first version ready?

Frontispiece

GS: The first version had been done. But when it was decided that the background and walls flanking the tapestry were to be white, I knew that the colour could be much brighter. Green and white seemed to be a good, fresh kind of combination, the one against the other. And in certain areas I intended to utilise more complex and even brighter colour—as bright as I could make it.

Later alterations and changes of idea with regard to the reredos, for example, did of course entail a number of adjustments on my part which weren't always easy to make. But I must repeat that, all the way along, Spence worked with me in as close a collaboration as possible.

AR: When visualising the tapestry *in situ*, you must have also had the congregation in mind. My impression is that the closer you get to the tapestry, the greater its impact. Was this deliberate?

GS: No. I believe that I have a certain sense of scale and that I can judge how a thing is going to look when large, even when I am working on a small scale. Whether I calculated accurately is not for me to say. As far as scale and impact are concerned, it comes within measurable distance of what I would have wanted. I did visualise that the tapestry, to be seen at its best, should be viewed from about three-quarters of the way down the cathedral. If one wants the total impact to occur immediately one enters the building, then one will be disappointed. This is partly due to the medium; due, too, perhaps to the wrinkling, which one hopes will eventually disappear. Although this is said to have a certain attraction, it does reflect a great deal of light, particularly in the background behind the central figure. This should appear to be quite dark: because of the wrinkling it is not in fact dark enough, and I believe that, if it were, the impact of the whole work would be much greater.

AR: Did you consider it a disadvantage that the tapestry, being created in a workshop, could not be viewed in its destined position until it had been finally completed, whereas with a mural or painting such as your altar-piece for St. Aidan's Church, Acton, you were able to make adjustments after the work had been hung *in situ*?

GS: I didn't so much need to see the tapestry in its setting because, during the whole course of the weaving, I had been used to looking at scale models of my design placed in a scale model of the cathedral. I was therefore fairly familiar with what the *general* effect was going to be. On the other hand, what I *did* want to do before it was put in its final place in the cathedral was to see the tapestry hung so that I could view the various relations of tonality at a distance and, if necessary, cause alterations to be made while the tapestry was still in France and within reach of the weavers, thus making adjustments possible. My wishes in this sense were also a duty to the authorities since it was underlined in my contract that I and the architect should be the final arbiters of the accuracy of the interpretation before they took delivery.

THE PROBLEM OF RELIGIOUS ART

AR: When referring to religious art in our time, I feel that very few genuine artists can be called "religious" artists. Compared with medieval times we live in a non-religious age and in my view, therefore, Christian art on purely traditional or sentimental patterns is no longer valid. For me, there are really only two artists, yourself and Rouault, who have consciously or unconsciously understood this and created religious works which have an immediate impact on the spectator. Now I know that it was a commission—for the Northampton Crucifixion—which led you to do your first religious painting on a large scale; but since then you have become what one would call a "religious artist" by continuing to work on sacred themes, from your Thorn Tree with its strong religious undertones to your Deposition, your Christ carrying the Cross, and then the three important commissions, for Coventry, Chichester and Acton. What I would like to know is how you relate this side of your creative work to the rest, how far it is predominant or merely a sideline, and how far all are bound together. I have in mind the other two main facets of your art—portrait painting and, above all, what is called your landscape painting. I know it is not landscape painting in the conventional sense, but this is the term generally used for it.

GS: Your question is a complex one. Had it not been for Walter Hussey, now Dean of Chichester, I think it most unlikely that I would have found myself embarking on a series of religious projects. And I cannot say that such attempts as I have made in any sense predominate over my other work, which is concerned, as you know, largely with the mystery of natural forms; neither can I admit to this commissioned work as being a sideline. What I have done was done freely from choice so that inevitably, perhaps more than I realise, it is bound up with my other work.

But since such commissions of the kind which I have undertaken are governed by specific requirements, they to this extent fall into a category totally different from that of my painting of "free" responses.

And what is a "religious" artist? I quote your own term. As I see him in the strict sense (though I wonder if this is the most truthful one?) he is someone who brings his skill and understanding to bear on the problem of giving expression to the tenets of an organised belief. Those who have done this best in the past have gained no doubt from their belief. But they seem to have excelled especially because, in addition to this, they were naturally good artists. But is it not a fact that the possession of such a gift may be held outside any organised faith?

I would like to quote Baudelaire on this subject. Writing on the Salon of 1859, he says: "Religious writers . . . naturally tend to make beauty dependent on belief and more than one religious writer has attributed to a simple lack of faith this difficulty of giving expression to the things of faith. This error could be philosophically demonstrated if the facts did not show us sufficient proof to the contrary, and if the history of painting did not offer us examples of impious and atheistic artists producing excellent religious works. Let us simply say that since religion is the highest *fiction* of the human mind . . . it will require the most vigorous imagination and the most concentrated efforts for those who devote themselves to the expression of its acts and its sentiments . . . The only concession to those who hold the theory of faith as a unique source of religious inspiration is that, at the moment of executing his work, the poet, the actor and the artist must believe in the reality of what he is representing, fired as he is by necessity . . ."

It seems clear to me that there are various kinds of artists who, whether believers or not, have produced or could produce what could be called religious art both to-day and in the past. It is claimed for Matisse, for instance, that he was not a Christian. Yet he was drawn to do the work at Vence. Slight though this is, it is imbued nevertheless with a certain religious feeling, as I believe are most of his very late works. But I am also thinking of others: Picasso, Goya and Rembrandt, for instance. These artists come to mind because deeply rooted in them there is a genius for expression, a largeness of spirit, great perspicacity and curiosity, to say nothing of technical invention and a passion close to the sentiment which could be called, properly I think, religious.

On the other hand, what can one say of those "religious" works in the period of the decline of understanding of the visual arts in the Church—for they are not religious at all. You say that we live in a non-religious age and this may be true, and superficially, at least, it does seem that the climate of religion does not seem very sympathetic to educated people to-day and this tends to isolate work in which the subjects are religious ones. But I have never disliked working outside my normal scope and it interests me to try and solve new problems. And since the opportunities to fill spaces in architectural settings are not so many, one is inclined to accept them when they come, not thinking too much of the problems of isolation, but only of the degree of excitement one can find in oneself. I welcome, yet fear, commissions at the outset. In accepting them one can lose a degree of the nourishment of one's feelings which one is used to taking for granted in one's "free" work. But a great deal depends on the patron and one is fortunate if he is one whose understanding develops alongside one's own. In any case, I try to do what seems natural to me.

AR: It seems to me that the special difficulty you have to face is the creation of religious images which are comprehensible and at the same time have an impact on a by-and-large non-religious community. In the case of Christian iconography, which has its certain canonic limitations, this is much more difficult than in the case of a work like 'Guernica', for instance, for which Picasso invented an entirely new imagery. As Anthony Blunt once said, 'Guernica' could be called the major religious work of the twentieth century, expressing a sentiment which was just as powerful in the 'thirties as Christianity was in the Middle Ages.

But, to revert to the problem of religious art in modern times, you would probably agree that the last great religious artist in England was Blake. And there is a certain sort of affinity between you and Blake because you were both engravers before you became painters and the work of both of you has a strong literary accent—in your case not in the same sense as with Blake, since you are not a poet, yet your painting has a definite romantic, literary connotation. I wonder whether Blake's religious art has played any part in your imagery?

GS: Not in this particular work. While I admire Blake greatly as a poet, my admiration for his paintings is incomplete. The things of Blake's which I admired in the past, and still do, range from the pastoral works—Dr. Thornton' *Virgil*, for instance—to the Dante drawings. The illustrations to the *Songs of Innocence* and *Songs of Experience* have beautiful passages, but are not to me wholly satisfying. Blake's religious paintings I find much less good and they fail partly by technical incompetence. To answer your question, it would not be true to say that I profited from his work in this instance.

AR: In your own conception of religious painting, suffering and torture must have preoccupied you greatly because not only do your non-commissioned religious works make their striking impact through the violent representation of suffering, as in your Deposition and Carrying of the Cross, but also in the tapestry you obviously chose to depict the Crucifixion in the bottom panel as opposed to scenes which had been suggested from the life of the

Virgin. And I just wonder if you confirm this feeling of mine, that you are extremely sensitive to those events in the Gospels which deal with suffering and cruelty and which in fact have a stronger impact that any other Christian images.

GS: There were reasons enough for me to feel the need for a tragic and sombre element at the foot of the tapestry in contrast to the rest. Moreover, having lived through the epoch of Buchenwald and the rest of twentieth-century violence and cruelty, it would not seem unnatural to find that one's consciousness had absorbed and been touched by these events. The subject of man's cruelty to man is, after all, a modern legend. But you must not think I am attracted to cruelty as such.

AR: I did say sensitive to it, not attracted to it.

GS: I must allow you to be the judge of that. One's mind certainly should be open to all the impressions which daily make their impact. It is true to say, however, that I believe it to be much more difficult to invent a valid equivalent for tenderness—which perhaps many of us would like to do. And whatever hazards normally might attend the expression of an equivalent of this quality, I cannot escape the feeling that they become far greater when church images are in question, because the Church in the main (and I am not speaking of any particular church), in associating itself for so long in modern times with an art of banal and empty sentimentality, would with rare exceptions be unlikely to tolerate new and vital conceptions in this field.

Consciously or unconsciously—the fault may lie in oneself—this is inhibiting. Even so it would not deter me, if the opportunity presented itself, from attempting to walk the tight-rope. But in doing so I would like to feel that I was able freely to find my own solutions.

AR: Am I right in thinking that the Church does exercise a certain restraint?

GS: In the sense which I have tried to make clear, I have sometimes felt a degree of restraint. Not that I want to give the impression that I do not accept certain restraints which are normally bound up with the expression of the tenets of a faith and under conditions of mutual understanding and perception. On the contrary, such restraint is, as I have said before, in the nature of a string to a kite. And I have been more lucky than unlucky in my dealings with ecclesiastical authorities. Moreover, it is a good thing to work sometimes in relation to architecture on a theme, the elements of which are laid down.

And of course, ultimately, it is the measure of one's power of expression if one can, while submitting to the rules, transcend them. Yet there is in my mind little doubt that, concerning certain religious subjects, there is sometimes an impediment—and a gulf—between that which one might like to do and that which so far would be acceptable.

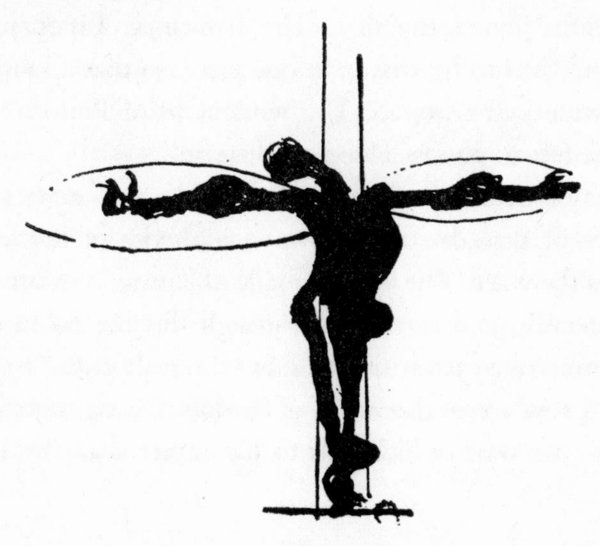

NOTES ON THE WEAVING

The Coventry Tapestry measures 74 feet 8 inches in height and 38 feet in width, and it weighs just over one ton. It is woven in one solid piece and is the largest tapestry in the world.

It was made in France by the firm of Pinton Frères at Felletin, near Aubusson, under the artistic direction of Madame Marie Cuttoli.

Tapestries have been woven in and around Aubusson since the Middle Ages; however, the average size of a large tapestry rarely exceeds 15 feet in height and 30 feet in length. Tapestries of greater dimensions than these were made in separate sections which were subsequently joined together. The Coventry Tapestry, on the other hand, was to be woven in one piece, so that a loom at least 40 feet wide was required. The workshops of Pinton Frères are one of the few to possess a loom of this size.

Tapestry is made up of coloured wools, known as wefts, woven into a set of threads stretched out lengthwise in the loom and known as the warp. The warp is made of cotton, reinforced at frequent intervals, and across and through this the coloured weft-threads are woven from side to side with a shuttle. The weavers work in a row across the width of the loom, each controlling the section of the warp which falls to his or her share by means of treadles.

The Coventry Tapestry was woven with a texture of 12 *portées* —a special tapestry-measure corresponding to 9 warp threads per inch. This measure indicates the density of the warp-threads only, since it is never the practice to give any count for the coloured wools forming the weft-threads or *duites* (a term signifying one passage of a weft-thread from left to right and back again from right to left on the loom).

The number of colours used exceeded 900. It is not possible to give an exact total since, in addition to the actual colours, threads of varying shades were on occasion mixed together to produce more delicate nuances of tone.

The wools came partly from Australia and were partly local French wools. They had a yarn-count (that is, a thread-thickness) of 20,000 and the threads used were double. They were specially spun at Roubaix.

The dyeing was done in the dye-workshops of Pinton Frères, using the water of the River Creuse, long famous for its excellent quality. The dyes themselves were fast, with a very high resistance to fading.

Twelve weavers were fully occupied on the weaving for over two years.* Apart from the weaving itself, a great deal of additional work was entailed by the immense size of the tapestry: this included the supply of a photographic enlargement of the cartoon in the full size of the tapestry; the numbering of the colours on this enlargement; the matching of the colours; and the sewing-up of the slits (i.e. the junctions of different areas of colour in the tapestry, which have to be sewn together after weaving).

* MM. Lepetit, Martinet, Chatard, Abracan, Lorcerie and Thuret; MMes. Habrial, Bacaud, Coste, Lorcerie, Pautout and Taudin; under the direction of Monsieur F. Genet.

SUMMARY OF DATES

1951	November 22nd	Spence writes to Sutherland, inviting him on behalf of the Reconstruction Committee to design the Great Tapestry.
	December 22nd	The Provost of Coventry, the Very Rev. R. T. Howard, draws up a statement on the subject-matter of the tapestry.
1952	January	Spence visits Sutherland at Villefranche to discuss the commission. As a result of this visit, Sutherland decides to accept.
1952–1953		Sutherland works on the design of the tapestry both in France and England.
1952	October	Trial panel of Calf woven by the Edinburgh Tapestry Co.
1953	September	Second trial panel, of a detail of Christ's head, woven by Edinburgh Tapestry Co.
	December 30th	The Right Rev. Neville Gorton, the then Bishop of Coventry, the Very Rev. R. T. Howard, the Provost, E. H. Ford, Chairman and Capt. N. T. Thurston, Secretary, of the Reconstruction Committee inspect with Spence the first cartoon at the artist's house, express their approval and invite him to continue.
1955	January 12th	Submission of second cartoon to Reconstruction Committee.
1956	January 3rd	After having written to her, Sutherland visits Mme Cuttoli at Cap d'Antibes to discuss the weaving.
1957	April 8th	Spence takes the new Bishop, the Right Rev. Cuthbert Bardsley, the Provost and the Secretary of the Reconstruction Committee to the artist's house to see work on revisions to the cartoon.
	September	Third cartoon submitted to the Committee at Coventry.
1957–1958	October to February	Sutherland revises certain sections of the third cartoon.

1958	February 20th	Final cartoon sent to France.
	February 27th	Sutherland and Spence visit Paris for discussions with weavers and Mme Cuttoli. Official contract signed with Pinton Frères. During the following months, work proceeded on the making of the photographic enlargements, the selection and dyeing of the wools, further work on the cartoon itself and, towards the end of the year, the weaving of a trial panel of the Eagle.
1959	February 27th	Sutherland and Spence visit Paris to inspect trial panel of Eagle.
	February 28th	Enlarged photographs spread out on floor of Garde Meuble Nationale and problems discussed. Sutherland already begins to demonstrate areas for revision on the spot and to outline plans for these.
1959–1961		Sutherland works at Menton in a disused store, keeping in frequent touch with the weavers. He redraws whole areas, simplifying and making corrections on the enlarged photographs.
1961	February 18th	After a visit to Felletin, Sutherland has the lower half of the cartoon returned to him to rework the skirt of the central figure.
	February 27th	Lower half of cartoon returned to Felletin.
	April 20th	Hands of Christ on photographic bands redrawn in gouache and sent to Felletin.
	May 18th	Sutherland visits Felletin to advise how the hands, now corrected in black and white on the photograph, could be arranged in relation to the original colour cartoon.
	December 22nd	Final working visit by Sutherland to Felletin.
1962	February 23rd	Sutherland visits Felletin to see the finished tapestry spread out on the floor of the local gymnasium.
	March 1st	Tapestry flown to England.
	May 25th	Consecration of the Cathedral.

APPENDIX I

Sir Basil Spence's invitation to Graham Sutherland

November 22nd, 1951

Dear Graham Sutherland,

I have just received permission from the Bishop and the Reconstruction Committee of the new Coventry Cathedral, to approach you with the object of having a discussion about designing the tapestry behind the high altar.

I may say that from the outset I designed the nave with the idea of closing one end with a great tapestry which would be the largest in the world and which could be woven by the Edinburgh Tapestry Company. I have discussed the manufacture with Lady Jean Bertie and they are all very happy that I have been permitted to approach you about the design.

But I must say from the start that there will be a great many restrictions. It has been decided that the tapestry should depict Our Lord in glory, but the figure is a very large one supported by the twelve apostles who would be immediately above the choir stalls. The great central figure will be behind the Bishop's throne. As in the Book of Revelation the figure should be golden, in a great vesica with the four winds and St. Michael commanding his hosts of archangels. You may not know, but this is the Cathedral of St. Michael and he should have special significance, being on the right-hand side.

The tip of the tapestry is 65 ft. from the ground and it is 44 ft. wide. After a good deal of discussion with the Bishop and other people, the seated figure of Our Lord should be about 30–32 ft. high, and it is very important that the face, hands and feet should be given special significance, as the hands and feet must show signs of the Passion.

I make a point of these restrictions as I would not like you to find later that you did not have a free hand, but I understand that this commission is very similar to those given many years ago for the church paintings. I personally am certain that a great artist should interpret these elements and from the first moment that I conceived this tapestry I thought of you as its designer.

You may not have seen the correspondence in the Press. This is a modern cathedral, and I have tried to contain in it understandable beauty to help the ordinary man to worship with sincerity, and I feel that the tapestry too should have a direct communication.

Please let me know if you would like to discuss the matter further and I will be very pleased to meet you in London or elsewhere. I understand that you are in Rome at the moment and I hope that this letter reaches you quite safely.

Basil Spence

APPENDIX II

THE COVENTRY CATHEDRAL TAPESTRY

A statement drawn up by the Provost on December 22nd, 1951, agreed with the Bishop on the same date, and communicated to Mr. Basil Spence.

This tapestry will be the dominating feature of the Cathedral for all the centuries to come. The congregation will have no choice but to see it all the time by night as well as by day. It is unlike a picture or window which people can choose to see or not.

The theme and subject matter must not be ephemeral but must present the timeless truths of the Christian Faith which are the same for all generations. They should be severely limited to scripture and within scripture to the main streams of Christian Faith. The tapestry must be theologically sound.

The artist-designer should be given great freedom in composition, colour, style, which will necessarily be of this generation. But if these are sincerely conceived and carried out, they will be beautiful for all generations.

The Subject

Christ The Redeemer, in the glory of the Father, shedding His Spirit upon the Church

(Christ being in the Glory of the Father, the scene is mainly in Heaven, with the lower part, the Church, in Earth.

In the Book of Revelation the Centre of Heaven is the Throne and One sitting on the Throne, and in the midst of the Throne the Lamb. It would not be theologically correct to place Christ alone at the centre of the Heavenly sphere leaving God the Father out. If God the Father is not to be represented at all, the scene must be on earth, e.g. the Resurrection or Ascension; but this leaves the Redemption of Christ incomplete, for it is not complete until the Glorified Christ bestows His spirit. But God Himself cannot be depicted in a tapestry, and the Lamb is not suitable for this tapestry.)

The tapestry in one unity of composition should depict the following four themes:

1. *The Glory of the Father*

   Though the form of God Himself cannot be depicted, yet the glory of His being must somehow be represented, e.g. Light ("light unapproachable") either above or around the figure of the Christ. The steps of the Throne reaching down out of the light could represent the Throne and Him that is sitting on it.

2. *Christ in the Glory of the Father*

   This will be the centre of the Tapestry. He may be standing as usually represented in Revelation.

   Or He may be seated, as in Hebrews and generally in Church Art.

   His hands and feet clearly show the signs of the Passion (the Redeemer).

   His attitude, though serene, should indicate His present active saviourhood of men on earth—e.g. He may be shown blessing, helping, ruling, giving the sacrament, especially drawing humanity up into Himself.

   His Face with dignity should inspire both reverence and love in the young and the common people.

   The figure of the Lamb as a small subsidiary subject might indicate the relationship of the seated Christ to the Lamb of Revelation.

3. *The Holy Spirit and the Church*

The apostles will represent the Church and Ministry.

The Holy Spirit will be represented by some symbol of the Spirit of Christ emanating from the figure of Christ and resting on the Apostles (e.g. the colour of flame might appear in the figure of Christ and be continued in or on to the Apostles).

4. *The Heavenly Sphere*

The space around on either side of the central figure of Christ will represent the Heavenly Sphere:

It will contain Angels and Archangels, especially St. Michael, and possibly other heavenly beings, though these should be familiar to the Christian mind.

It might also contain the worshipping multitude of the Saints triumphant. (N.B. The West Window will contain the saints in the life on earth).

It is important that the angels should be represented as not only occupied with the worship of heaven but also with "succouring and defending us on earth" (Collect for St. Michael and All Angels).

These four main themes will afford the artist almost infinite scope for creative imagination. It will be for him to unite them into one composite whole.

APPENDIX III

Letter from the Very Rev. R. T. Howard, Provost Emeritus of Coventry

The Provost's House, Coventry
April 17th, 1957

My dear Mr. Sutherland,

When I think of the responsibility we have put upon your shoulders in designing the tapestry, I feel guilty for having laid such a burden on anyone! Yet your spirit in tackling it has all along been so fine, that I am sure you will be more than equal to it.

It was very satisfying to see how the new design has advanced on the previous one, excellent though that was.

The bottom panel remains a problem. I feel quite certain that the subject must be one of the four chief scenes from the life of the Blessed Virgin Mary as recorded in the Bible—the Annunciation, the Visitation, the Mother and Child, the Virgin Mary and St. John standing by Christ upon the Cross. I gathered from you that you feel the need of the tragedy of the Cross to balance the glory above. This seems to indicate the last of the four subjects. It is important that our Lord should be seen *upon* the Cross, or it becomes the Pietà. You will remember the letter that Bishop Neville Gorton wrote to you about that in January 1954. He there agreed with me that it would be better not to have the Pietà, but either the Annunciation or the Mother and Child. As you feel that these two are difficult to deal with in view of the Glory above,

I feel that Bishop Gorton would have been willing, as I am, that the "Standing by the Cross" would be right. Our present Bishop agrees with this view.

Some inspiration will come to you for the treatment, I am quite sure.

With my best wishes to you and your wife,

R. T. Howard

COLOUR PLATES

Plates I to X reproduced by permission of the Coventry Cathedral Council

VI

VIII

X

CATALOGUE OF BLACK AND WHITE PLATES

Unless otherwise stated, all these studies were formerly in the collection of Mrs. Graham Sutherland and are now reproduced by courtesy of the Redfern Gallery, London (by arrangement with Marlborough Fine Arts, Ltd.).

1 STUDY FOR CHRIST IN GLORY Conté crayon, $7\frac{5}{8}'' \times 5\frac{3}{4}''$

One of the early sketches done at the beginning of 1953, in which the artist was seeking to establish the general proportions for the central figure in relation to the whole area. At this time the tapestry was not yet intended to reach to the ground, so that no allowance is made for the lower section it later on acquired.

2 CHRIST IN GLORY WITH TWO EMBLEMS

Oil and gouache on brown paper, $24\frac{1}{2}'' \times 22''$

Another early study attempting to rationalise the pose, here with the arms raised. Right from the beginning Sutherland was playing with the possibilities of three alternative poses: with the arms raised, horizontal or lowered. This composition has no mandorla and contains only two of the four emblems.

3 TWO STUDIES FOR THE WHOLE TAPESTRY

Pencil, $8\frac{1}{4}'' \times 10\frac{1}{8}''$

One of the earliest attempts done towards the end of 1952, immediately after receipt of the first scale-model of the cathedral. According to Sutherland, these drawings were made after he had visited Venice for the first time, because by then he had seen Torcello with its shallow, low-pitched roof. Spence too went to Torcello, and it may have been this which led him in turn subsequently to raise the ceiling of the retro-choir, which he had originally intended to be flat, into a shallow inverted V.

Sutherland made only two drawings previous to those illustrated here—one done in red chalk on the back on an envelope and another, now destroyed, which he made to fit into the first scale-model of the cathedral.

4 STUDY FOR WHOLE TAPESTRY Gouache, $17\frac{3}{4}'' \times 13\frac{1}{2}''$

One of the early sketches done before the first cartoon, exploring further the composition of the left-hand drawing on Plate 3.

The proportions, however, are still more squat than in the final cartoon, showing that this was made before the architect narrowed the shape of the retro-choir. It nevertheless contains a panel below Christ in the mandorla bearing indications of a Deposition, so that by now it had been decided that the tapestry should, in fact, reach to the floor.

5 STUDY FOR WHOLE TAPESTRY Gouache, $46\frac{3}{4}'' \times 25\frac{1}{2}''$

Collection: H.M. The Queen

Done shortly before the second cartoon, in order to try out a different pose with the hands folded in the lap. The lower section now contains a triptych with a Pietà in the central panel, the Annunciation on the left and the Visitation on the right. The position of the emblems is the reverse of that in the final version.

6 STUDY FOR CHRIST IN GLORY Oil and gouache, $32'' \times 18''$

One of the more finished preparatory studies for the second cartoon, done at Roquebrune in 1954. The arms are now outstretched horizontally, consequently the panels containing the four emblems have been lowered. In the bottom section there are indications of the proposed triptych depicting the Annunciation, a Pietà and the Visitation in accordance with the request of the Reconstruction Committee for subjects suitable for a Lady Chapel.

7 THE SECOND CARTOON (without lower section)

Oil and gouache on board, $79\frac{1}{2}'' \times 43\frac{1}{2}''$

Shown together with the first cartoon (see Frontispiece) to the Reconstruction Committee, who had to make a choice as to whether they preferred the arms raised or lowered. Sutherland argued in the direction of this second version as being less sentimental. This version already contains the figure of the man between Christ's feet and also the chalice built into a form of pedestal, but the mandorla has been excluded. The sleeves have been enlarged in order to fill the space created by the raised arms. The cartoon shown to the Reconstruction Committee had a triptych at the base with a Madonna in the centre. This was subsequently removed and a Crucifixion similar to that in the final tapestry substituted in the centre panel. There is an indication of the arrangement of the original lower panels in the study for this cartoon (see Plate 6), but this illustration shows the cartoon without the lower section.

The scale-model of the cathedral exhibited in Brussels in 1958 contained a colour photograph of this second cartoon.

8 THE THIRD CARTOON

Oil, gouache and cloth collage on board, 79″ × 43¼″

This cartoon was submitted to and approved by the Reconstruction Committee in September, 1957. It no longer exists in this state, as Sutherland himself was not satisfied and stripped off certain details which he overpainted to form the final version. The figure and face of Christ were very largely altered and in many respects simplified. The panel at the bottom depicting the Crucifixion remained unchanged in the final version.

9 THE FINAL CARTOON

Oil, gouache and collage on board, 79″ × 43¼″

Collection the Coventry Cathedral Council

The actual maquette which was sent to Felletin and from which the weavers worked. It differs from the tapestry itself only in certain details which Sutherland redrew on the enlarged photographs made from it for the benefit and guidance of the weavers.

10 FIGURE OF CHRIST Charcoal and ink, 8″ × 4¾″

This was in fact a study of a natural leaf form. According to Sutherland, it seemed to him the kind of shape that he wanted for the figure and, whether done consciously or unconsciously, the crucifix motif is traceable in it.

11 SEATED FIGURE Conté crayon and ink, 12″ × 6″

One attempt to get some kind of basic form for the drapery, probably done by Sutherland throwing a piece of cloth over his shoulder and drawing it from his reflection in a mirror.

12 CHRIST BLESSING

Pen, pencil and gouache on tracing paper, 4½″ × 2¼″

One of the innumerable drawings done by Sutherland of the figure of Christ in various positions with various treatments, in his attempts to arrive at some kind of final conception for the form this figure was to take. Here the hand is raised in blessing, the other arm is hidden beneath a cape and the legs are crossed as in certain Romanesque representations. One could say that this drawing belongs to the sketches done with the purpose of eliminating certain traditional poses in order to arrive at a new interpretation (see also Plate 15).

13 STUDY FOR CHRIST — Gouache on tracing paper, 11″ × 7″

An intermediary study between the second and third cartoons with the motif of the open skirt adopted for the latter. Sutherland was here seeking to get away from the conventional silhouette of quasi-Roman or -Gothic drapery. This is, in fact, a paraphrase of a priest's vestments with oriental undertones.

14 FIGURE OF CHRIST — Pencil and ink, 12″ × 4″

Another concept for the pose of Christ's figure with extreme simplification of the upper part, the arms being covered by a cape. This pose is reminiscent of Egyptian sculpture.

15 CHRIST SEATED — Oil on board, 55½″ × 20″

Collection Mr. & Mrs. John Hunt, Howth, Co. Dublin

An early finished painting containing a number of elements which Sutherland subsequently discarded as being too reminiscent of traditional representations, such as the classical drapery and the crossed feet (see Plate 12). It is dated 1954–5.

16 STUDY FOR CHRIST — Chalk and gouache, 9¼″ × 5⅛″

A drawing from which Sutherland worked for the final cartoon. The skirt is very similar in both.

17 FIGURE OF CHRIST — Ink, chalk and wash, 15½″ × 8½″

An attempt to incorporate elements, notably the skirt, drawn from a draped lay figure. This was pursued further in a more complex form in the drapery study illustrated on Plate 20.

18 FIGURE OF CHRIST — Pencil, crayon and ink, 12″ × 4½″

A study for the drapery done from a clay figure on which pieces of cloth were experimentally hung. A standing figure with an opening, to see what could be done by enveloping a figure with a cloth. At one time Sutherland thought of using a partially nude figure for Christ (see also Plate 15).

19 SEATED CHRIST Pen and pencil on tracing paper, $15\frac{3}{4}'' \times 8''$

Another study for the drapery with a certain feeling of the figure underneath. The shoulders in this case were going to be free and bare with a diagonal band of drapery over them like a cape (see Plate 15). The arms are in fact a study for those in the first cartoon.

20 STUDY FOR LOWER PART OF ROBE

Ink, pencil and gouache, $7\frac{5}{8}'' \times 5''$

According to Sutherland, this was an attempt to see what would happen if he particularised this part of the figure much more by actually accepting the shapes formed by a real piece of cloth. Although fascinated by the result, he decided to abandon it as being too complicated and therefore liable to detract attention from the face.

21 FIGURE OF CHRIST WITHOUT HEAD

Gouache, pencil and ink, $15\frac{1}{4}'' \times 9\frac{1}{4}''$

A study done from a draped clay figure. It bears some relation to the first cartoon with the arms lowered, but the diagonal band of drapery is similar to that in Plate 19.

22 HEAD OF CHRIST Gouache and ink, $18'' \times 12''$

Collection Mrs. Alice Hunt, New York

The earliest study for the head of Christ, done in 1952, this is a free transcription from a reliquary in Limoges enamel which Sutherland saw exhibited in Paris. It belongs to the studies which transcribed traditional representations, not with a view to being used but in order to form a vocabulary of what had already been done.

23 HEAD OF CHRIST Gouache, $9'' \times 4\frac{3}{4}''$

Done as a sort of working drawing for the head, very soon after the first cartoon, as an experiment in type and proportion. Though differing in expression, it became the basis for the three future cartoons.

24 HEAD OF CHRIST Detail from first cartoon (Frontispiece)
Gouache, 78″ × 43″

Although Sutherland retained this head virtually unchanged in its shape and proportions in the final cartoon, he considerably altered the expression, feeling that this one was too sentimental. He was looking for something that was both more human and also stronger.

25 HEAD OF CHRIST Gouache on board, 39½″ × 23½″
Collection Lady Honor Svejdar, Dublin

This painting is almost identical with the head in the tapestry itself (Colour Plate III).

26 STUDY FOR ARM WITH DRAPERY
Conté crayon on lined tracing paper. Detail from a drawing 7½″ × 6″

Probably done from the artist's own arm reflected in a mirror with a piece of material draped over his shoulder.

27 STUDY FOR SLEEVE
Gouache, ink and chalk on lined tracing paper, 14¼″ × 7½″

One of the intermediate studies for the sleeve done before Sutherland decided to leave the forearms bare.

28 STUDY FOR HAND Conté crayon, 7¼″ × 3¾″

Like Plate 29, this drawing was done preparatory to the final cartoon, probably from the artist's own hand in a mirror.

29 STUDY FOR HAND
Pencil and red chalk on tracing paper, 10″ × 4½″

Also one of the drawings done from Sutherland's own hand, preparatory for the final cartoon. This particular study shows traces of the stigma which appears in the tapestry.

30 STUDY FOR HAND AND SLEEVE
Ink, chalk and gouache, 13″ × 5″

This was also done before the final cartoon was finished. The pose is slightly suggestive of a priest's hand raised in blessing.

31 STUDY FOR HAND

Pencil and wash touched with white, 20″ × 8¼″

Done after Sutherland received the photographic bands and after the weaving had started, when he decided that certain details must be redrawn. This particular study is the one he transposed, virtually unaltered, on to the photographic enlargement for the weavers, with only slight adjustments in the length of the fingers.

32 STUDY FOR FEET — Gouache, pencil and ink, 6¼″ × 8⅝″

As with the hands, Sutherland on seeing the enlarged photographic bands decided that the feet as well must be redrawn and started to make a number of diagrams in attempts to plan the most satisfactory lighting. According to him, one of his problems was created by the frontal view, which made it difficult to arrive at a shape which was both interesting and realistic. He wanted this frontal pose, however, since to him it seemed an essential part of the effect of the whole work. He therefore did a series of studies such as this one, analysing the planes of the foot and ankle with a view to solving the problem of the frontal position, mostly from his own feet in a mirror.

33 STUDY FOR FOOT — Charcoal, 11″ × 8½″

Another drawing in the same series as Plate 32, done from the artist's own foot reflected in a mirror.

34 DETAIL FROM A GROUP OF TWO STUDIES FOR THE FIGURE OF THE MAN BETWEEN CHRIST'S FEET

Pencil, 10″ × 6″

The legs in this particular detail were also done from life, probably by the artist using his own legs reflected in a mirror. For this motif Sutherland wanted absolute rigidity and symmetry. This drawing probably dates from 1957/1958.

35 STUDIES FOR MAN: EMBLEM OF ST. MATTHEW

Pencil, ink and chalk, 11″ × 8½″

According to Sutherland, the most difficult problem for him was to find a satisfactory symbol for St. Matthew. This was not because of the normal difficulties associated with drawing a figure in any specific position, but because he wanted to avoid the usual clichés associated with supplication and in particular with representations of this subject. In the first cartoon (Frontispiece) the emblem of St. Matthew is shown in a very severe, kneeling pose. The artist was dissatisfied with this solution and in these sketches was trying out a variety of different ideas.

36 STUDY FOR MAN — Pencil, ink and wash, 10″ × 8½″

Done for the same reason as the sketches on Plate 35. Sutherland here used a certain degree of distortion with a view to finding a distinctive pose which would take the place of facial expression.

37 STUDY FOR MAN — Ink, wash and white chalk, 8½″ × 9″

Sutherland found the idea of a winged man unsympathetic. This was one of his experiments showing the wings in different positions. The formal, squatting pose has very strong oriental connotations.

38 STUDY FOR MAN — Pencil, ink and wash, 10″ × 7″

This drawing is almost identical with the final version used in the tapestry (see Colour Plate V), depicting the Man as if he were coming out of a window. It is above all by movement and distortion that the eagerness of expression at which the artist was aiming is achieved.

39 STUDY FOR CALF: EMBLEM OF ST. LUKE

Conté crayon and pencil, 10″ × 8″

Of all the motifs in the tapestry, the design for the emblem of St. Luke remained one of the most consistent throughout the various phases. Sutherland felt that in the first cartoon he had achieved a satisfactory relation between the image and the panel; it had seemed to work out fairly naturally and he did not feel the need to explore further variations. This drawing was done in order to fix the pose and expression.

40 STUDY FOR CALF — Watercolour, ink and chalk, 13″ × 9¾″

A more detailed study with slight variations in the pose and a more realistic treatment of the wings which was subsequently discarded.

41 STUDY FOR CALF — Gouache on cardboard, $26\frac{3}{4}'' \times 12\frac{1}{4}''$

A more definitive study, fixing the subject in relation to the proportions of the panel it occupies. Very close to both the version in the first cartoon (Frontispiece) and the one in the final tapestry (Colour Plate IV).

42 STUDY FOR LION: EMBLEM OF ST. MARK

Gouache, $11'' \times 13\frac{5}{8}''$

The only version in which Sutherland gave the beast four wings, according to the letter of the Book of Revelation. He abandoned this idea, however, since it could not impart the note of realism which he wanted. The small squares on the face were an attempt to convey the feeling of mosaic. This study has a strong red background—indeed many of the studies done at this period have arbitrary coloured backgrounds, which do not necessarily bear any relation to the colour which the artist intended finally to use.

43 STUDIES FOR LION

Conté crayon, ink and watercolour, $12\frac{3}{4}'' \times 9\frac{3}{4}''$

Parallel with his sketches exploring the various styles in which the emblems might be depicted, Sutherland also made a number of studies from life in Maidstone Zoo and also from magazine photographs. This is one such study based on nature.

44 STUDY FOR LION — Gouache, $10\frac{1}{4}'' \times 9\frac{1}{2}''$

A free study from a mosaic in the church of St. Apollinare in Classe, Ravenna. The lion is holding the Gospel, which was the traditional representation of the emblem of St. Mark in Byzantine and medieval art. Sutherland abandoned this motif as he did not wish to be tied in any way to traditional iconography.

45 STUDY FOR LION — Gouache, $14'' \times 8\frac{1}{2}''$

This was the actual representation of the lion used on the second cartoon illustrated on Plate 7. At some stage it was cut out of the cartoon and now exists as a separate study. The pose differs only in minor respects from the final solution in the tapestry itself (Colour Plate VII) in which, however, a yucca tree was added alongside, making the panel more square. The expression in the final version also gained greatly in strength and force.

46 STUDY FOR EAGLE: EMBLEM OF ST. JOHN

Gouache on brown board, $10\frac{1}{2}'' \times 6\frac{1}{2}''$

One of the realistic sketches for the eagle, showing the bird in flight. At this stage Sutherland was experimenting with many different poses in his attempts to get away from the heraldic connotations. Finally, however, he decided that the bird in flight did not harmonise with the other elements in the composition. Also, in his view, it was insufficiently interesting as a shape when seen from a distance.

47 STUDY FOR EAGLE — Gouache, $10\frac{3}{4}'' \times 7''$

An intermediary study done between the second and third cartoons. The bird is shown about to alight, almost hovering, but the whole pose is more heraldic, although the head is realistic and is based on the life study illustrated on Plate 48.

48 HEAD OF EAGLE — Conté crayon, $6'' \times 5''$

A purely realistic drawing, done from the life in Maidstone Zoo.

49 HEAD OF EAGLE — Pencil, $7\frac{3}{4}'' \times 5''$

Another study from nature, done possibly from a stuffed specimed in Maidstone Museum. The expression bears a close kinship with the final version in the tapestry (Colour Plate VI).

50 ALTERNATIVE STUDY FOR EAGLE

Pencil and gouache, $8\frac{1}{2}'' \times 6''$

An isolated study of a representation which Sutherland developed no further. It has the attributes of a gryphon and derives from Egyptian and other ancient sculpture which Sutherland had seen. It is also the only study which shows rudimentary suggestions of a landscape background.

51 STUDY FOR EAGLE — Gouache and white chalk, $5\frac{1}{8}'' \times 6\frac{3}{4}''$

Another version showing the bird in flight, as in Plate 46.

52 STUDY FOR EAGLE — Gouache, ink and chalk, $6\frac{1}{4}'' \times 9\frac{1}{2}''$

A drawing done probably from life, seeking to analyse the essence of a bird of prey's expression. According to Sutherland the eagle owl is one of the birds he finds most fascinating, and this study is in fact of an eagle owl.

53 STUDY FOR EAGLE Gouache, ink and chalk, $6\frac{5}{8}'' \times 8\frac{5}{8}''$

A study worked up from a quick pencil sketch following Plate 49. Whatever the pose was to be, Sutherland decided that all the expression must be concentrated in the head of the bird, a simplification of the construction of the beak and eyes, as being the eagle's salient characteristics.

54 STUDY FOR EAGLE Gouache, ink and chalk, $19\frac{1}{2}'' \times 9\frac{1}{2}''$

One of the later studies, already very close to the final solution as used in the tapestry (Colour Plate VI).

55 STUDIES FOR ST. MICHAEL Ink, chalk and wash, $13'' \times 9\frac{3}{4}''$

Like the emblem of St. Luke, the panel containing St. Michael remained more or less consistent throughout the various stages. In his first version already Sutherland depicted St. Michael fighting the dragon, "who is called the devil and Satan" (Revelation), in the form of two human beings wrestling. In this sketch both heads are shown in outline only. In the final tapestry a dragon's head takes the place of the human head (Colour Plate VIII).

56 STUDY FOR THE CRUCIFIXION Pencil, $10'' \times 6''$

The motif of the Crucifixion has preoccupied Sutherland ever since the commission for St. Matthew's, Northampton. This pencil drawing was in fact done before he received the commission for the tapestry, and he calls it "a sort of afterthought on the Northampton Crucifixion".

57 STUDY FOR THE CRUCIFIXION Conté crayon, $15\frac{3}{4}'' \times 9''$

This drawing was also made before the Coventry commission, but Sutherland referred to it and also to the drawing on Plate 56 for the Crucifixion panel at the foot of the tapestry.

58 STUDY FOR THE CRUCIFIXION Ink and wash, $7'' \times 7''$

One of the most moving studies for this subject. The Gothic swing given to Christ's body emphasises His suffering.

59 STUDY FOR THE CRUCIFIXION WITH FIGURES

Chalk, ink and wash, 8″ × 7½″

The large number of exploratory drawings and studies for the Crucifixion shows Sutherland's extreme concern with this subject which he finally chose for the lower panel in the tapestry. This sketch was done at a time when he was contemplating a more full-scale Crucifixion with Mary Magdalen at the foot of the Cross and the Virgin supported on the right.

60 STUDY FOR THE CRUCIFIXION WITH FIGURES

Chalk, ink and gouache, 9⅛″ × 10½″

A more elaborate working-out of the idea of a full-scale Crucifixion with figures hinted at in Plate 58. On the left has been added the mounted figure of Longinus piercing Christ's body with the spear. Also the weeping sun and moon used in the final version appear here for the first time.

61 STUDY FOR THE CRUCIFIXION WITH FIGURES

Ink and gouache, 10¾″ × 10½″

Another composition for a Crucifixion with figures. The horizontal bar of the Cross is now curved, and this was used in an even more marked manner in the final version for the tapestry (Colour Plate X). Sutherland was, of course, familiar with Picasso's *Crucifixion* and admits his debt to it. In both this study and Plate 60 the central figure of Mary Magdalen at the foot of the Cross refers to a *Deposition* which Sutherland painted in 1946 (see Robert Melville, *Graham Sutherland*, London, 1950, Plate 15).

62 CHRIST ON THE CROSS Gouache, 20½″ × 15″

One of the many studies done in order to establish a pose for the figure of Christ. The head, in this position, is not dissimilar to that in the Crucifixion by Sutherland in St. Aidan's Church, Acton.

63 CHRIST ON THE CROSS Gouache, 9½″ × 5½″

Again an attempt to explore the possibilities of a different position—a position much more of movement. Sutherland found, however, that this pose did not seem right in relation to the design of the tapestry above and reverted therefore to a more static pose in his final version. In fact, this pose can be seen to form a second position by turning the study on its side.

64 STUDY FOR THE CRUCIFIXION

Ink, chalk and gouache, $10\frac{1}{2}'' \times 10\frac{3}{4}''$

The artist's intention here was to see if he could achieve a completely symmetrical central figure, having a group of mourners only on the right and leaving the rest of the space as a tremendous blank, to be read as either sky or wall, counterpoised simply by the black square, or window, at the top left, which would have contained a white cross. This study bears a close resemblance to Sutherland's large *Crucifixion* done in 1962/1963 for St. Aidan's Church, Acton.

65 CRUCIFIXION WITH SUN AND MOON

Ink, chalk and gouache, $10\frac{1}{2}'' \times 10\frac{3}{4}''$

This study approaches the final version in its main elements; the ancillary figures have been abandoned and the sun and moon assume a prominent position. In the final and most accomplished version (Colour Plate X) Sutherland added a bier behind the Cross with a cloth draped over it ready to receive Christ's body; also a dark curtain hanging down behind Christ's figure to stress the whiteness of His body.

66 STUDY FOR TRIPTYCH

Ink and gouache, $7\frac{1}{8}'' \times 10''$

One of a number of studies made when it was proposed by the Cathedral Authorities that the bottom part of the tapestry should be filled with a triptych illustrating scenes from the life of the Virgin. The centre panel was to contain a Pietà, flanked on the left by the Annunciation and on the right by the Visitation (see Plates 5 & 6). The curved shape at the top of this drawing, which was to make a base for the feet of the central figure of Christ, represents an idea Sutherland had at this time of using a nature form transformed into a kind of supporting pedestal, similar in shape to the left-hand form in his painting *Monuments against a Landscape* (see Douglas Cooper, *The Work of Graham Sutherland*, London, 1961, Plate 123c).

67 PIETÀ AND VISITATION Gouache, ink and chalk, $6\frac{3}{4}'' \times 10\frac{1}{2}''$

Studies for the centre and right-hand panels of the proposed triptych at the foot of the tapestry.

68 STUDY FOR PIETÀ

Ink and gouache on tracing paper, $14'' \times 15\frac{3}{4}''$

In his first cartoon Sutherland filled the lower section with a central panel depicting a Pietà at the foot of the Cross. In this he gave the body of Christ greater prominence than to the Virgin.

69 STUDY FOR PIETÀ

Ink, chalk and gouache on brown board, $7\frac{1}{2}'' \times 9\frac{1}{4}''$

A sketch exploring a grouping of the figures different from that illustrated in Plate 68. This was used for one of the studies for the whole tapestry (Plate 5).

70 STUDY FOR THE VISITATION

Ink, chalk and watercolour, $11\frac{5}{8}'' \times 8\frac{7}{8}''$

Sutherland took the pose for this study from a photograph in *Life* magazine of two Indian women greeting each other.

71 STUDY FOR THE VISITATION

Ink, chalk and gouache, $11\frac{3}{4}'' \times 9\frac{1}{8}''$

A more rhythmic variation of the study on Plate 70.

72 STUDY FOR THE ANNUNCIATION

Ink, chalk, pencil and gouache, $11\frac{1}{4}'' \times 9\frac{1}{4}''$

The only extant study for this subject. Sutherland felt very strongly that there was a wide discrepancy between this theme and the spirit of the main subject-matter of the tapestry. For this reason he developed it no further and, on his urging, it was agreed that the lower part of the tapestry should contain a central panel only, depicting the Crucifixion.

5

6

7

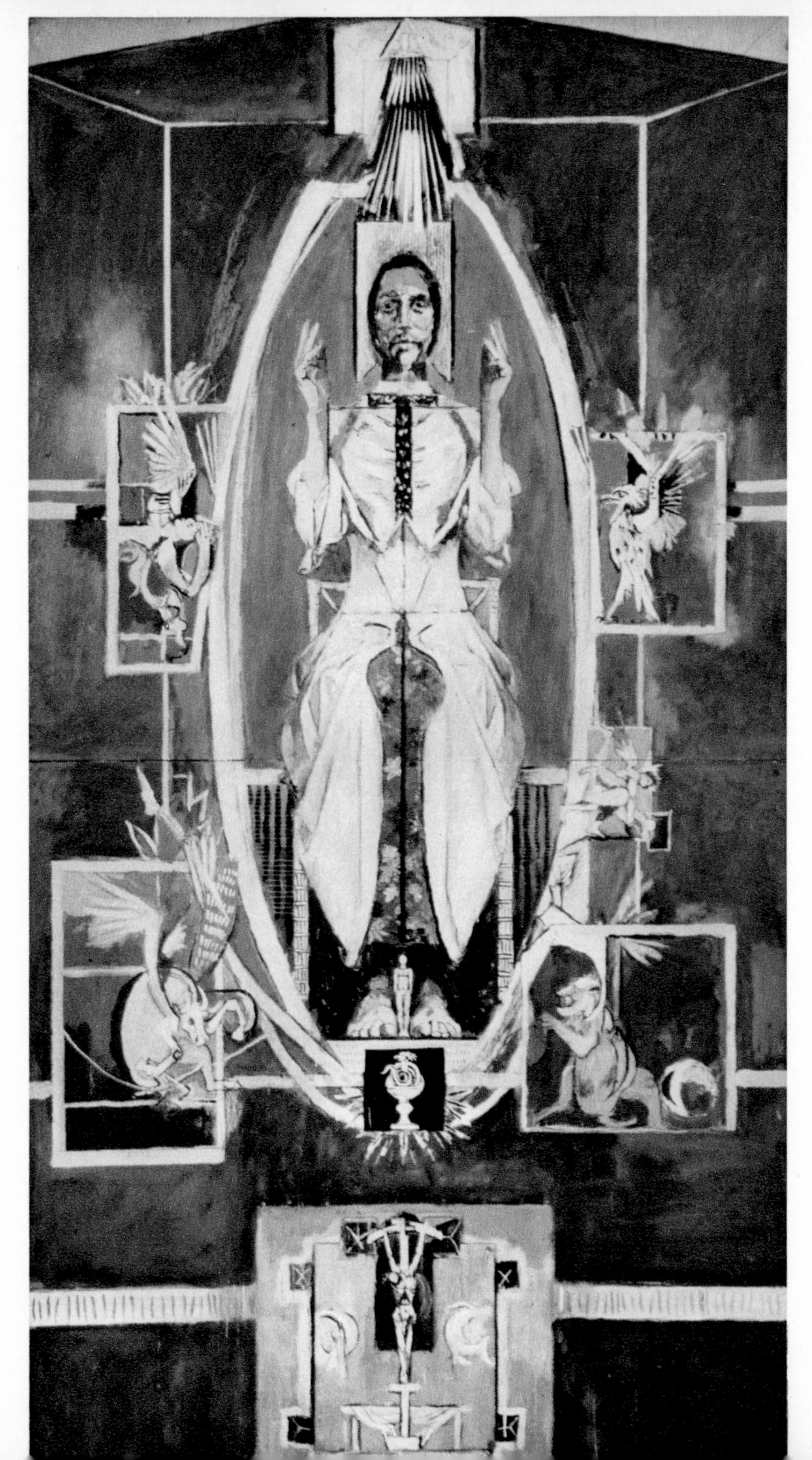

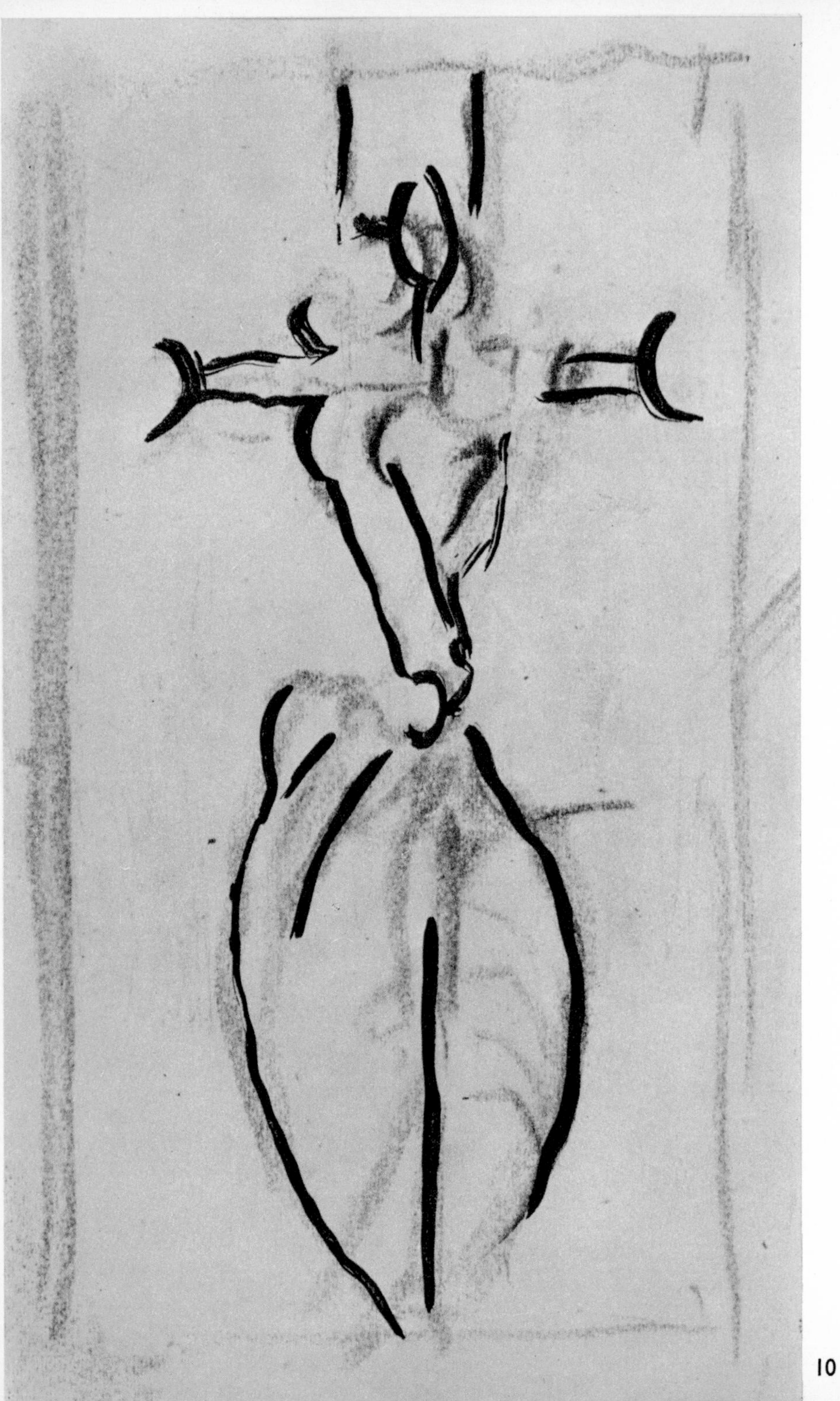

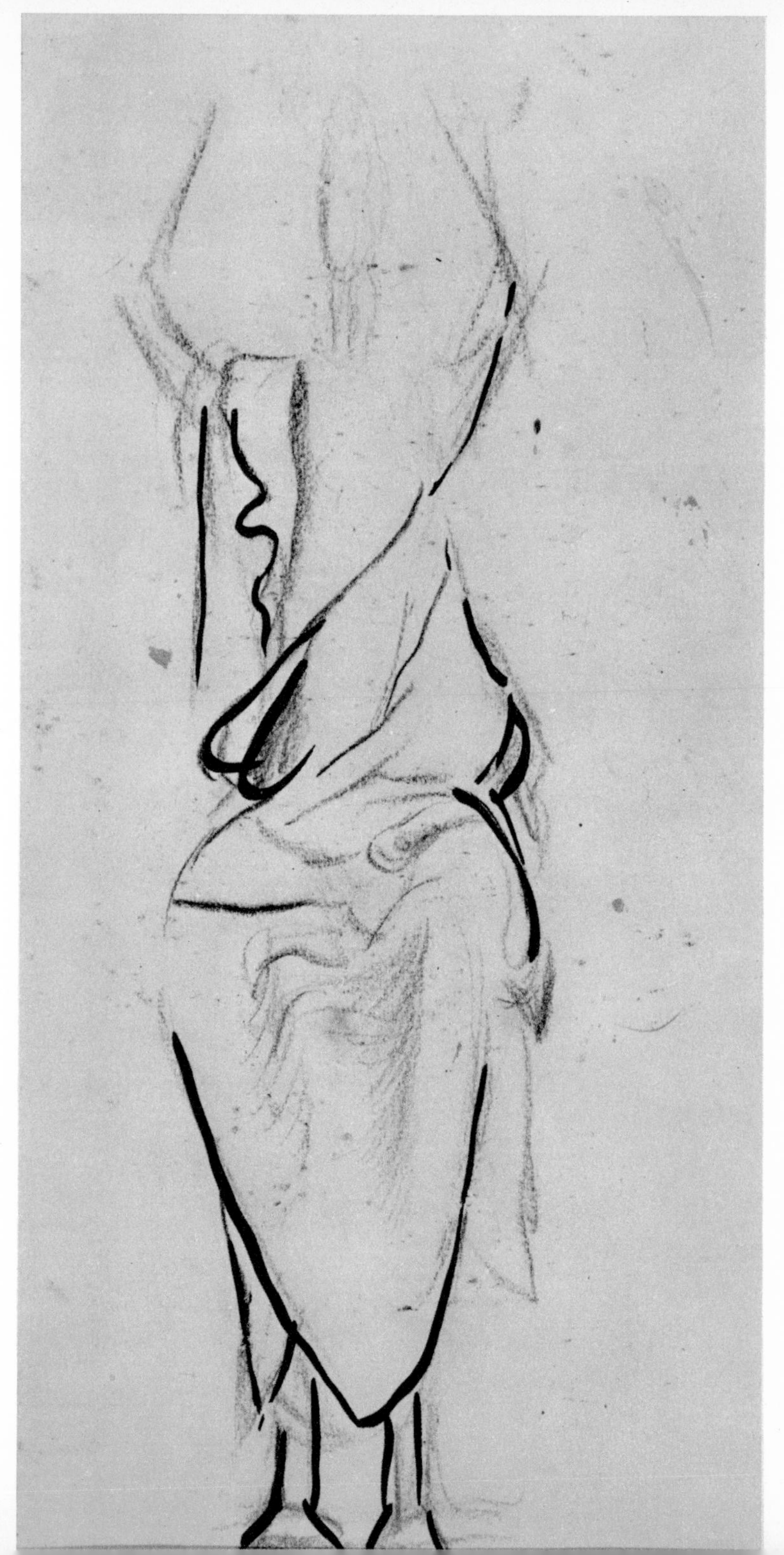

11

12

13

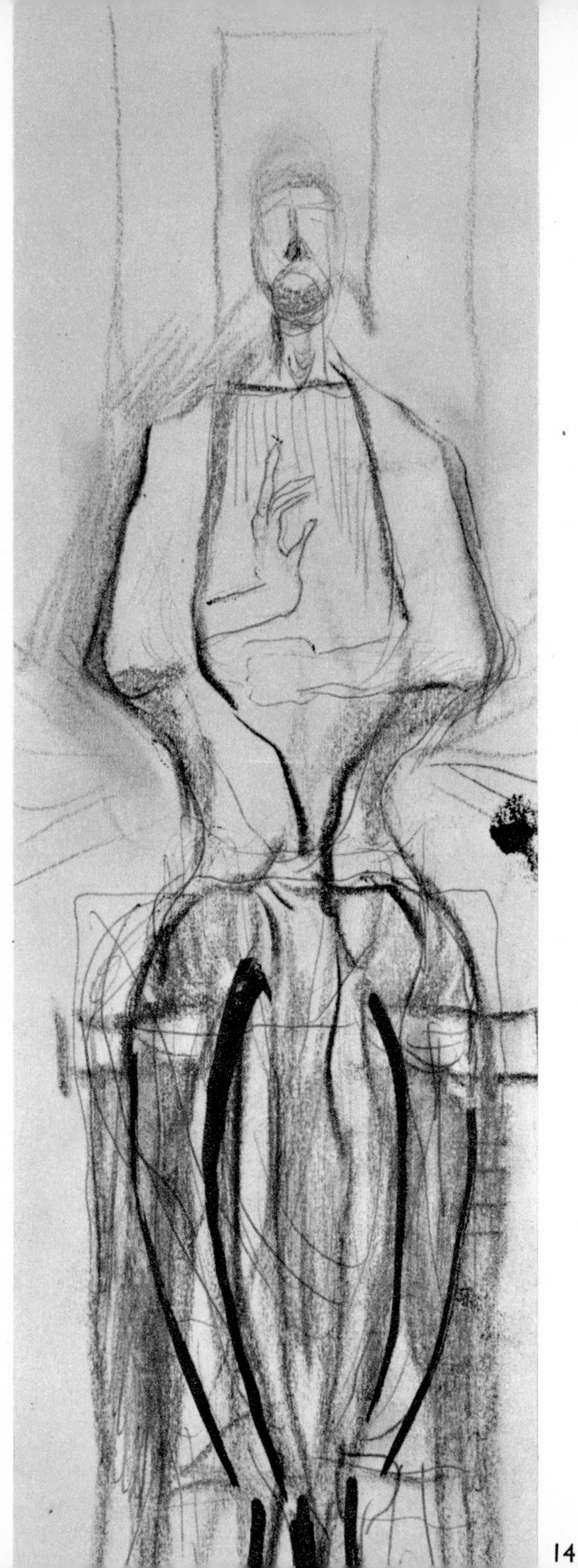

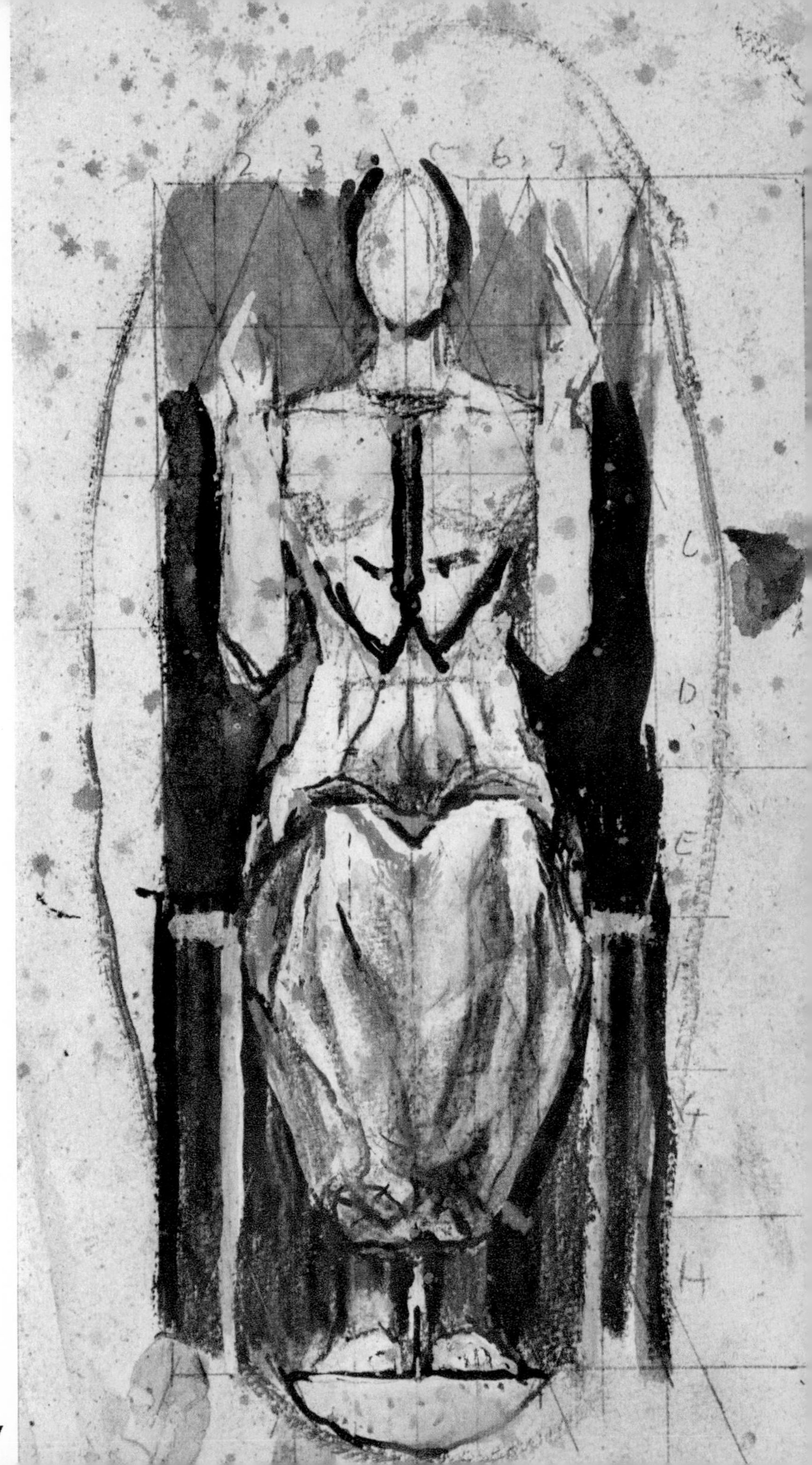

17

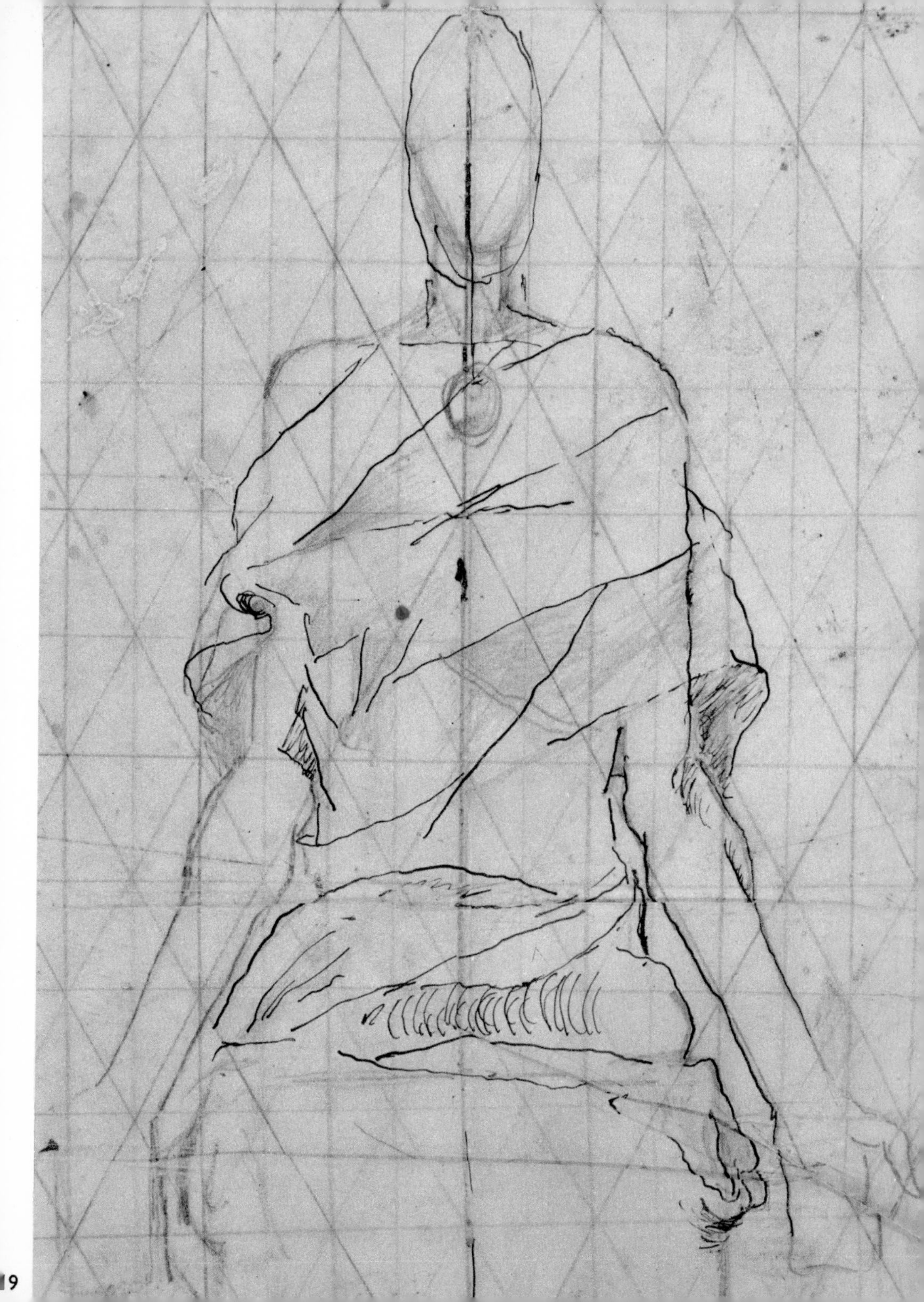

25

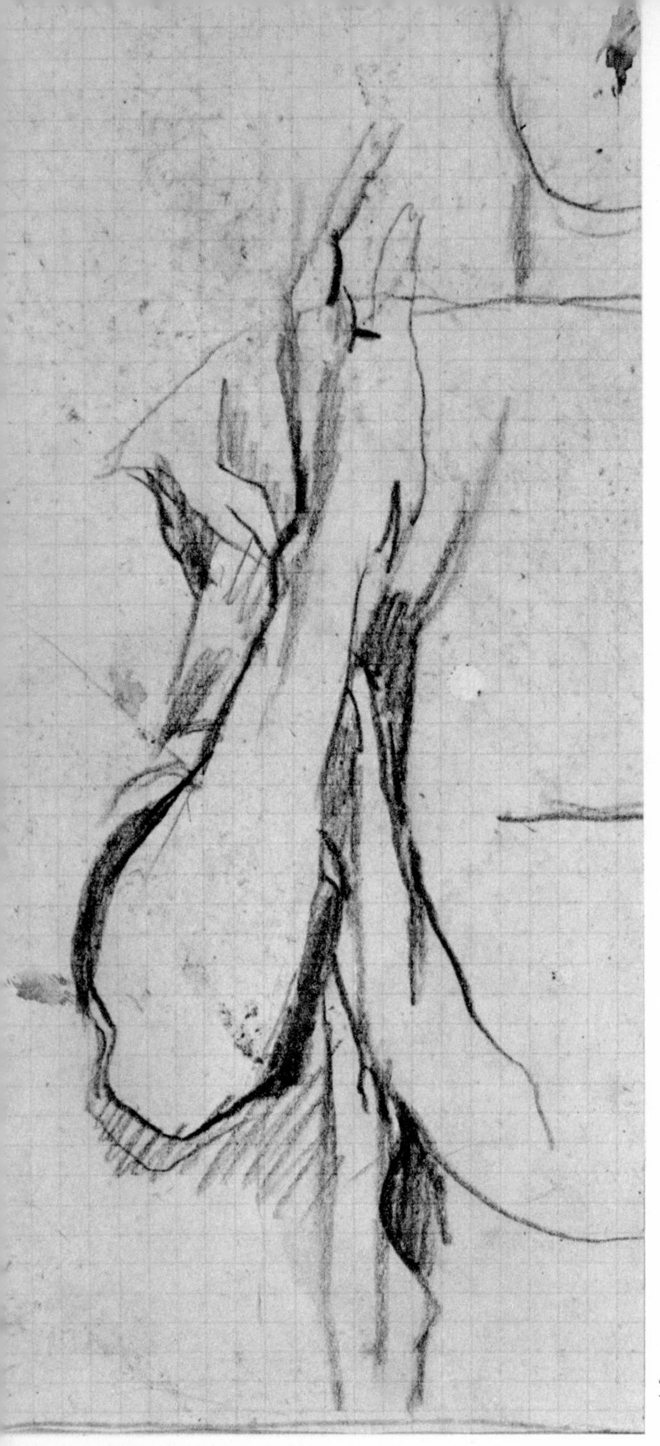

26

Study

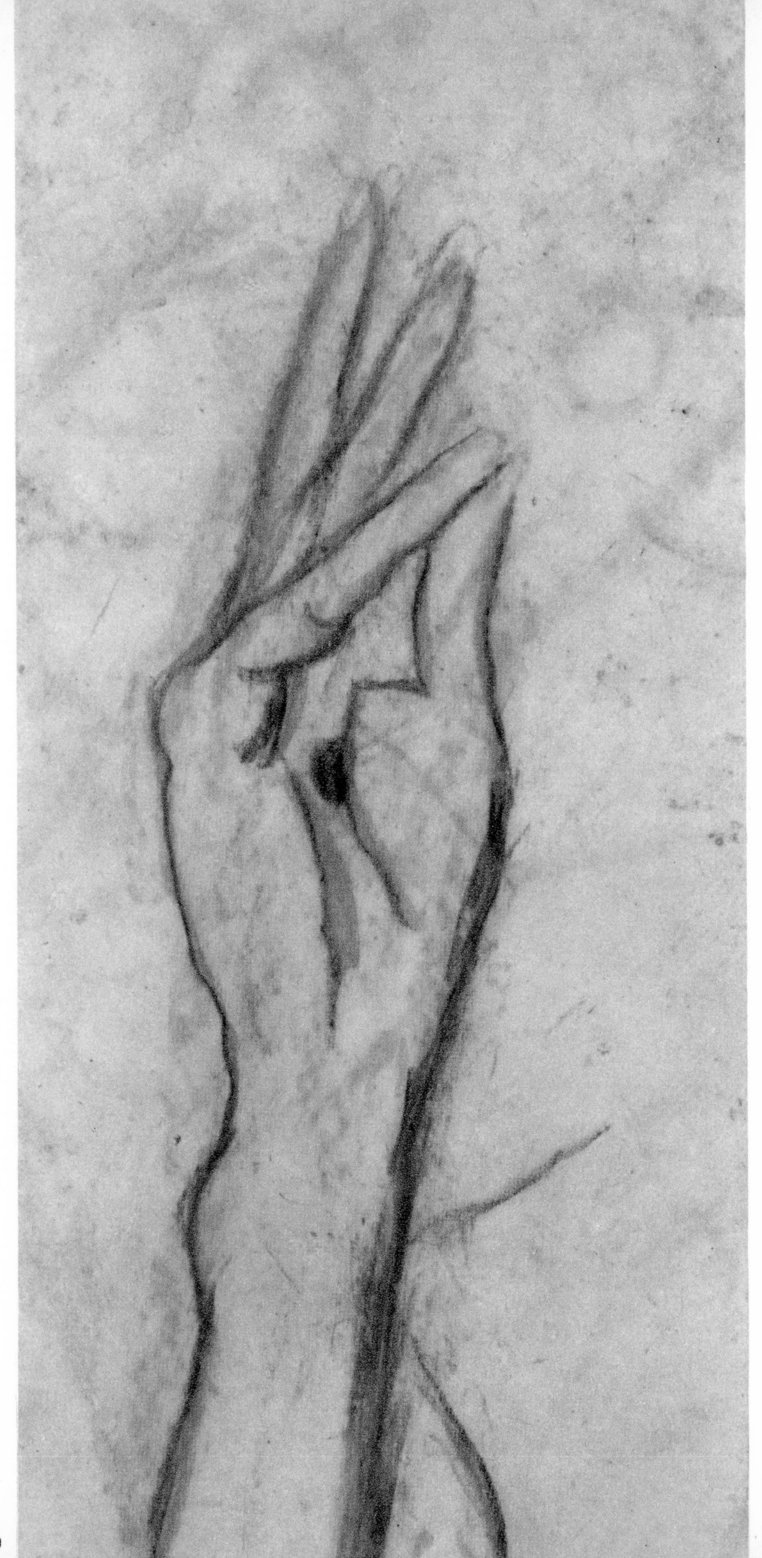

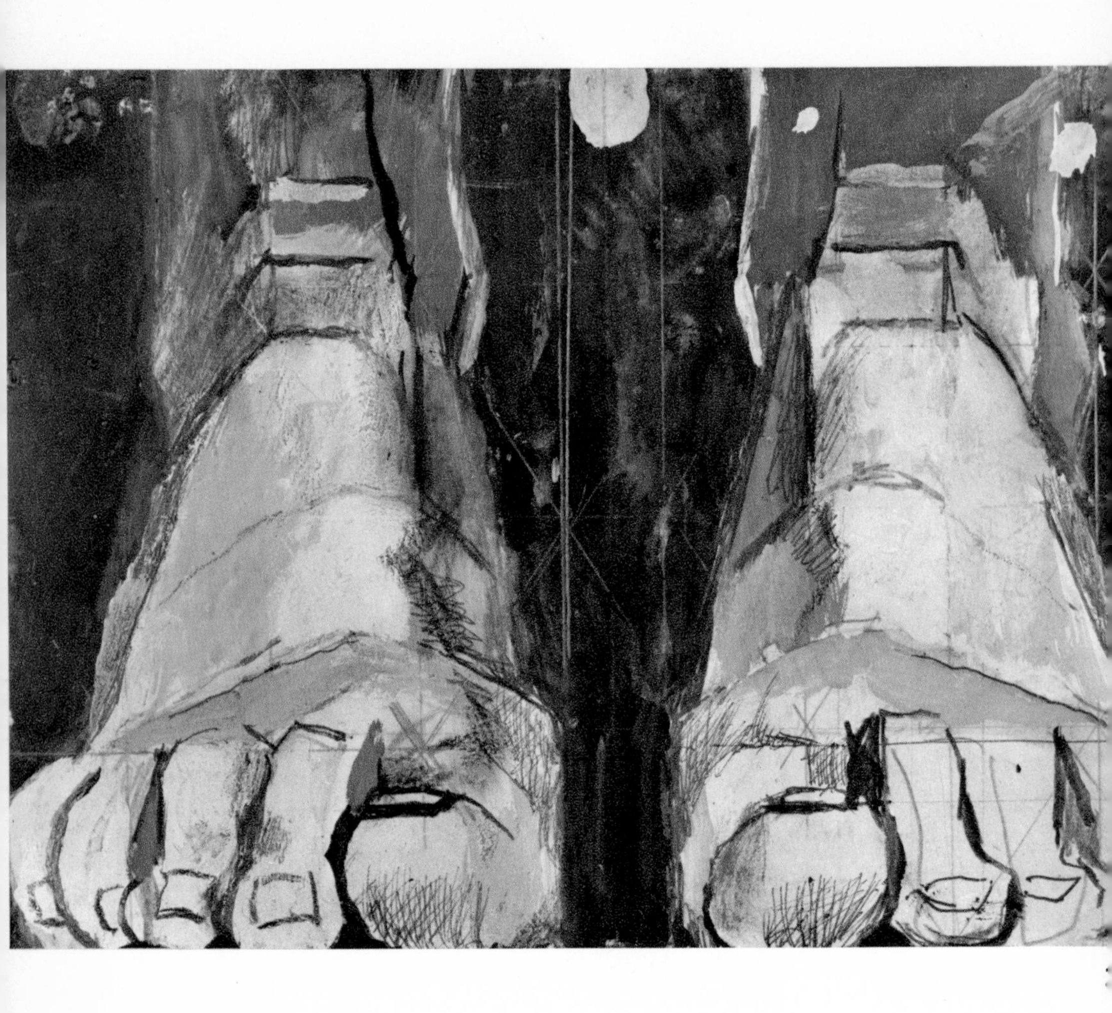

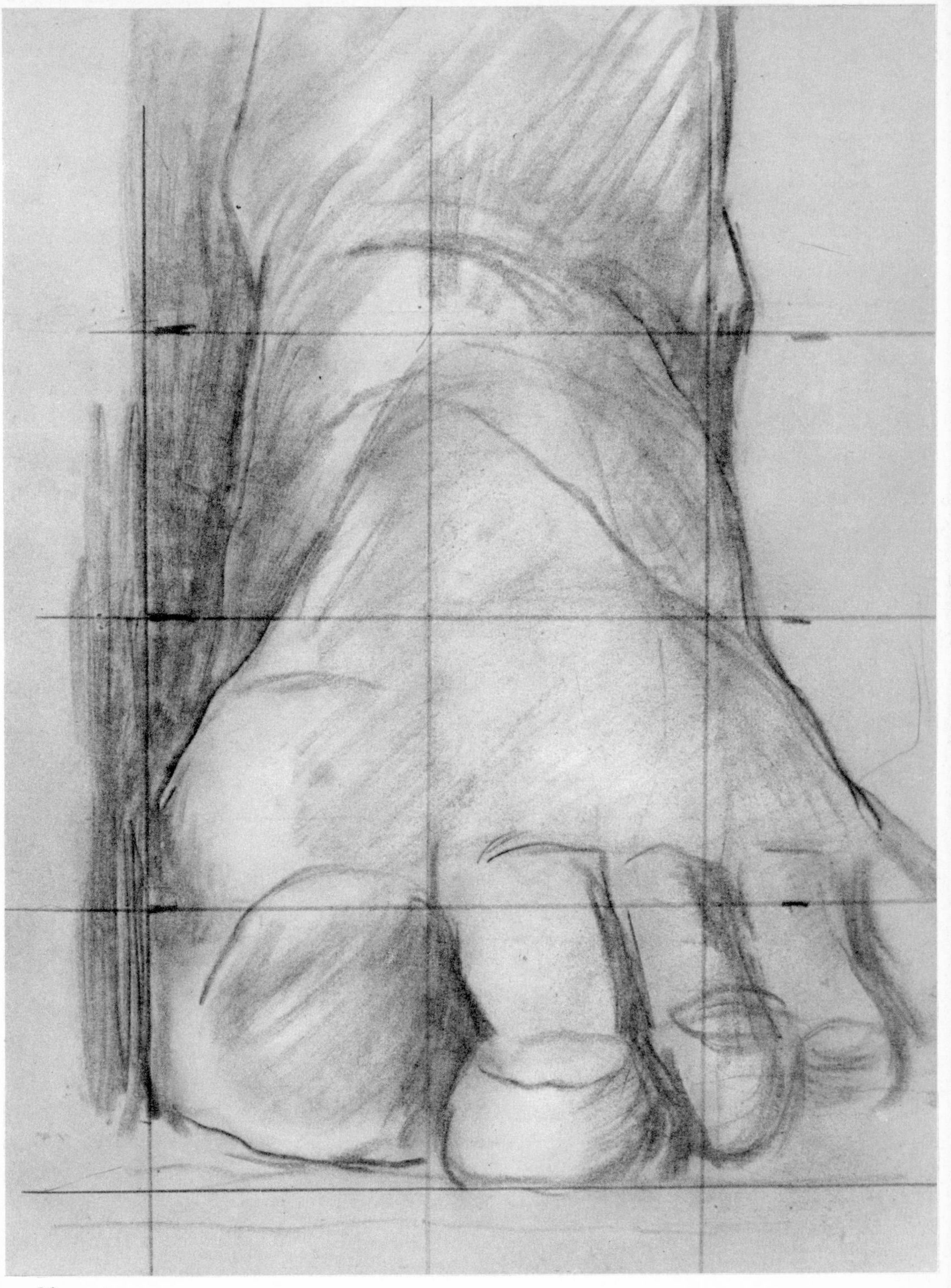

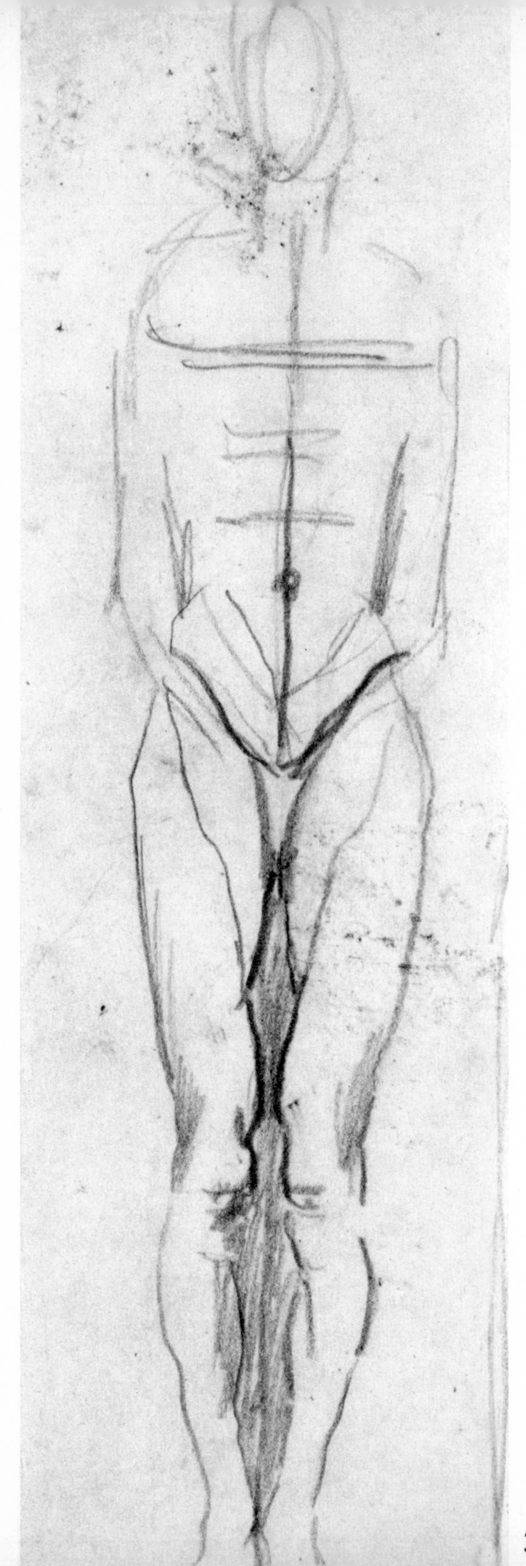

37

39

41

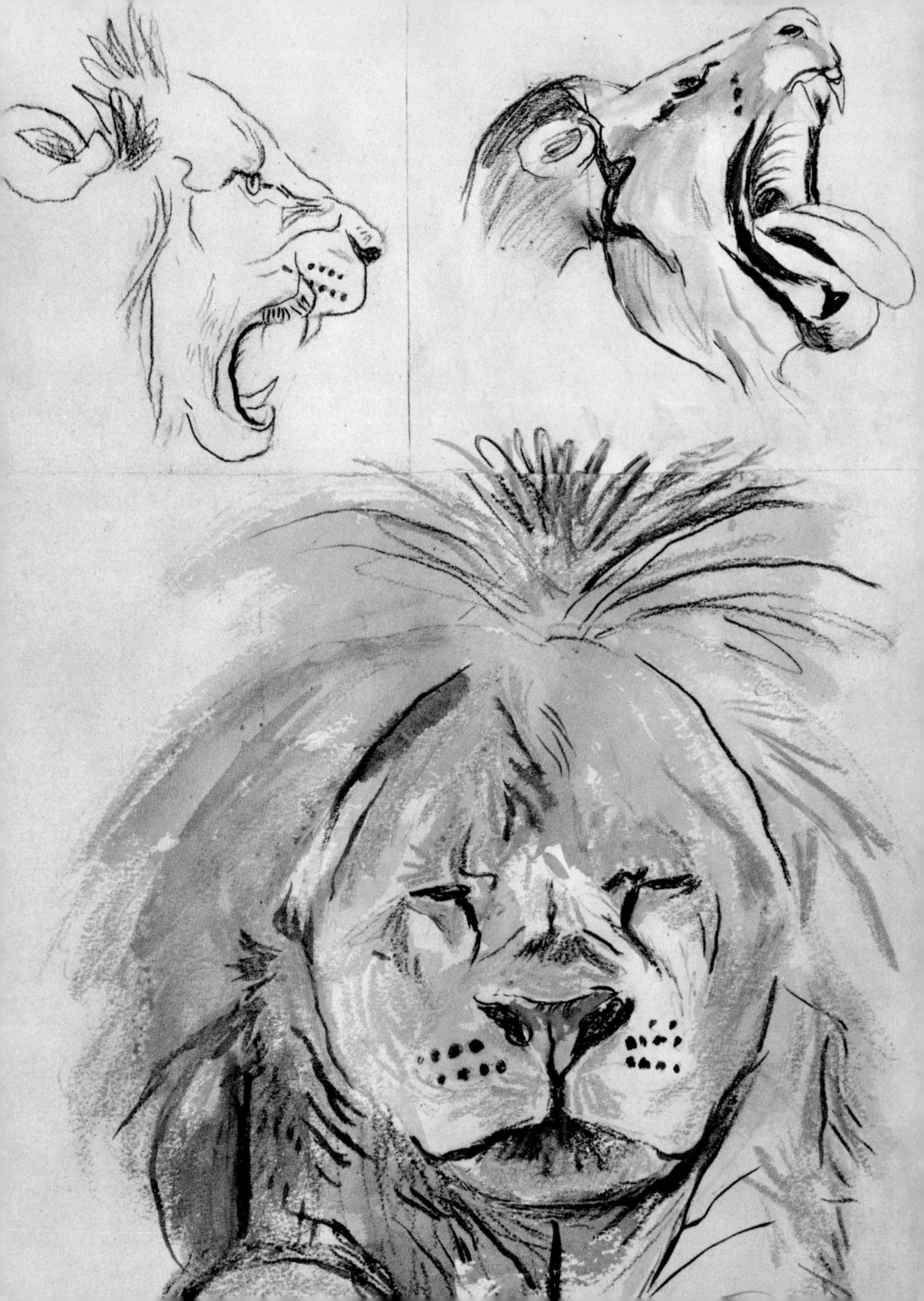

45

48

49

alternative
Study for Eagle

51

5

53

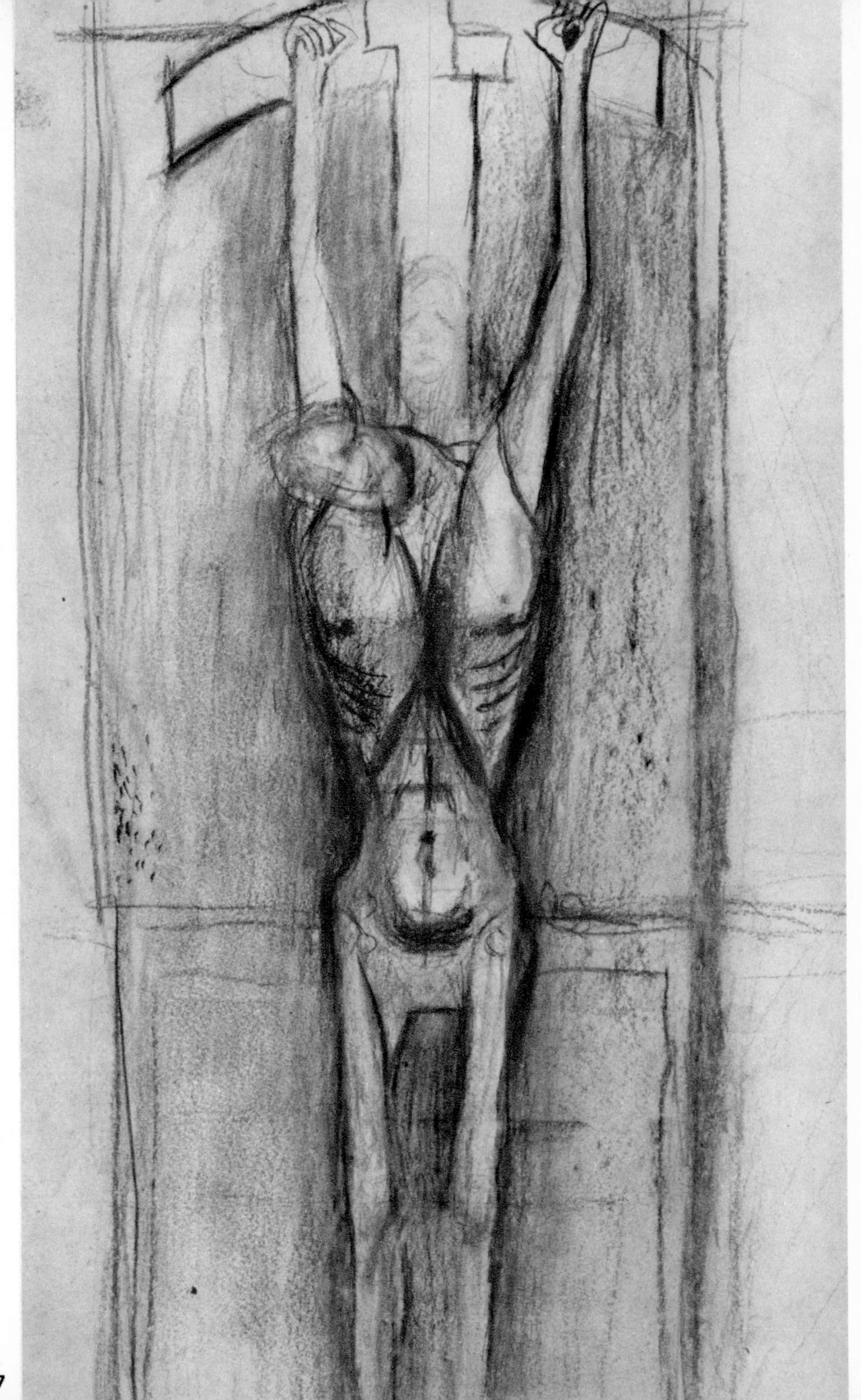

57

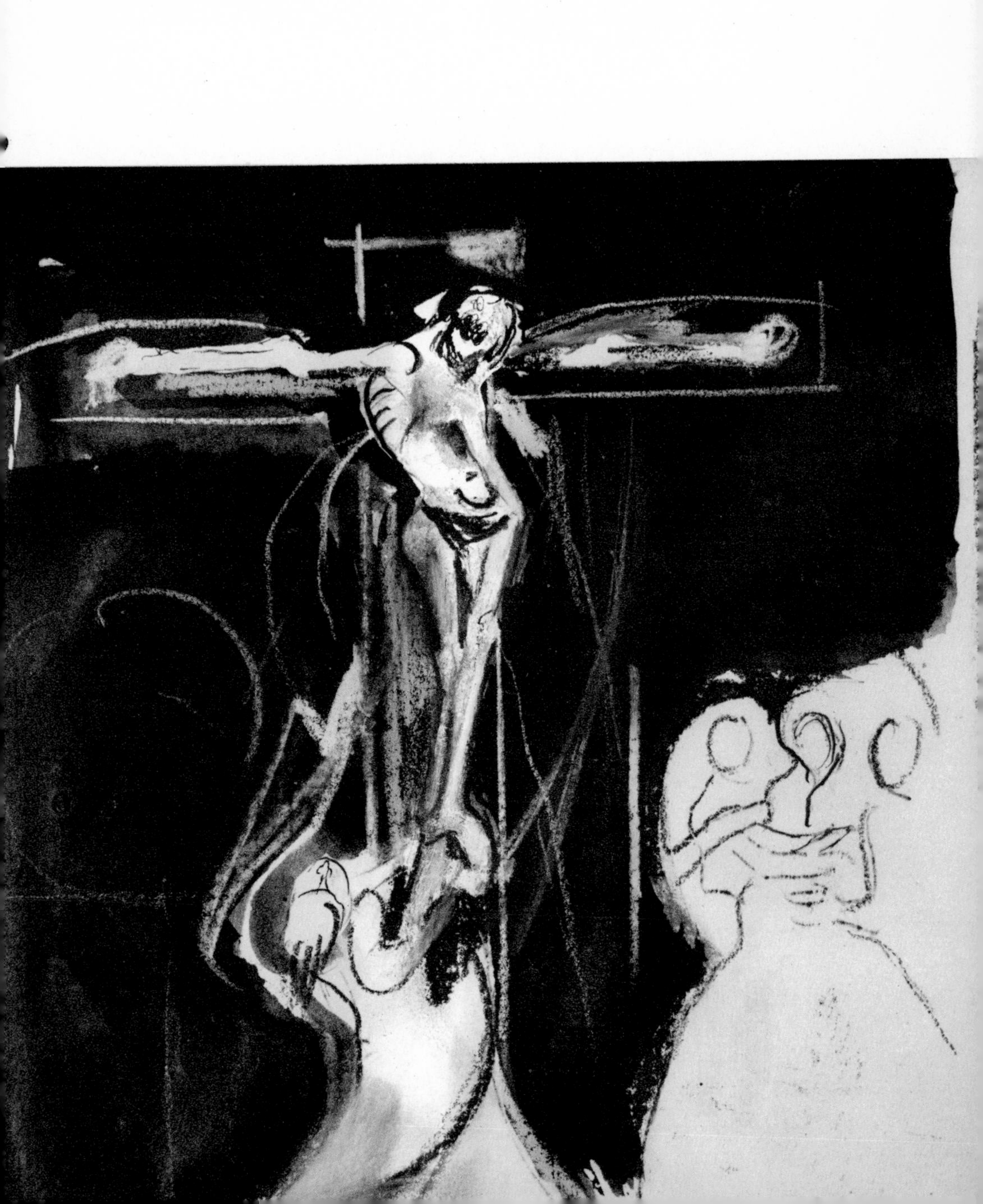

60

I

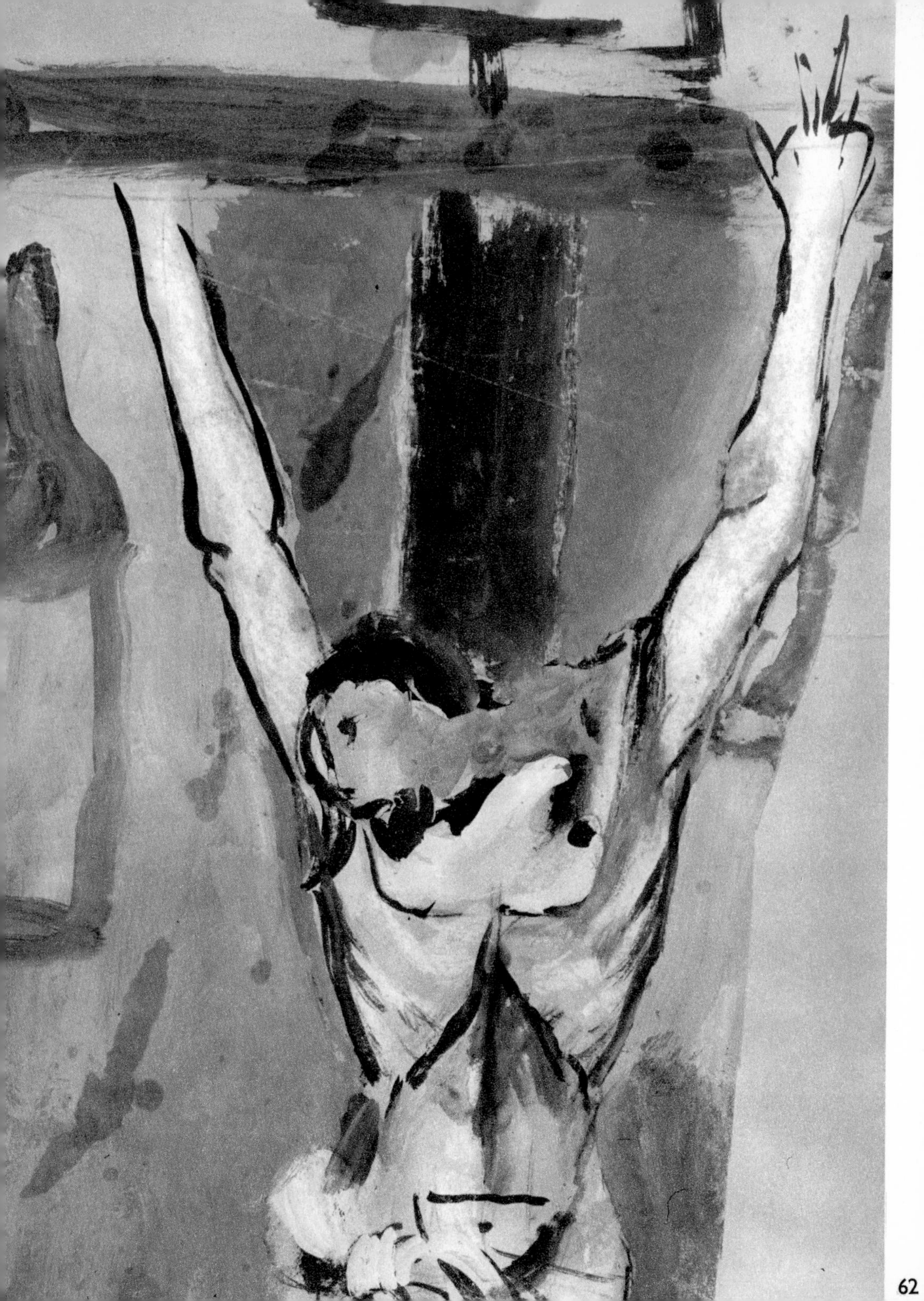

5

6

67

69